EPIC

Eternal Purpose In Christ

Also by Pastor Tom Carter

Identity Crisis

Six Steps to the Throne

Jesus Rant Vol. 1

Crystal Star

Hazard

All scriptures are from the King James version of the Holy Bible, unless otherwise noted. MSG stands for the Message Bible. AMP stands for the Amplified Bible.

Thomas W. Carter
www.jesusrant.com

ISBN: 978-0-9859564-7-9

For Worldwide Distribution, Printed in the U.S.A.

First Printing: 2014

Dedication

This book, as always, is for Jesus. I didn't write it. He wrote it through me.

This book is for my spiritual father, Pastor Eric King, who coined the phrase, "EPIC destiny," and lit a fire under me to finish the "Answer Trilogy."

And for my natural father, Pastor Dennis Carter,

who always has my back no matter what.

I love you guys.

This book is for you if you've ever wondered "Why am I here...?"

Contents

Introduction

You are not an accident. You are here not only on purpose, but for purpose and by purpose! God made you specifically. And He made you specifically... you! It doesn't matter "in the natural" how you came about. It doesn't matter where you came from, or where you are right now. Because you have an EPIC destiny. You have an Eternal Purpose In Christ!

Ok. As simply as I can put it, your destiny is to be conformed into the image of the Lord Jesus Christ. And, as mind blowing as this may seem... your destiny was completed over 2,000 years ago on the cross at Calvary! The journey--the Christian life--is not conforming into the image of Jesus. The journey is finding out what the image of Jesus is and what it means to already be conformed into that same image!

Romans 8:29 says, *"For whom he did foreknow, he also did predestinate to be conformed to the image of his Son, that he might be the firstborn among many brethren."*

Now let's define some terms here: "Foreknow" - (G4267) "To know beforehand, that is, foresee, ordain, know before." God knew you before you were ever even a gleam in your parents' eyes. Jeremiah 1:5 says, *"Before I formed thee in the belly I knew thee; and before thou camest forth out of the womb I sanctified thee, and I ordained thee a prophet unto the nations."* You were known, and you had a purpose before you were even born. You were ordained to live a life, and a more abundant life at that!

"Predestinate" - (G4309) "To limit in advance, that is, predetermine, determine before, ordain." There's that word "ordain," again. You were ordained. You were chosen. You were predetermined to something specific. God knew you, and had a plan for you, right from the beginning.

"Conformed to" - (G4832) "Jointly formed, that is, similar, fashioned unto." You weren't born in the image of Jesus. You were born in the image of Adam. And a seed can only produce after its own kind. An apple tree can only make apples. Adam, a human, could only make more humans. Something had to happen to change you--or conform you--into the image of Jesus. What happened was the cross!

"Image" - (G1504) "A likeness, that is, statue, profile, or representation, resemblance." This word is interesting, because it causes a lot of confusion. Are we the "image" of Jesus, or are we Jesus? I've already written two books showing how and why I believe we ARE Jesus. We are the perfect representation of Him, just as He was the perfect representation of His heavenly Father during His earthly ministry.

The key is the end of the verse. The key is realizing that Jesus is the firstborn Son of a new, incorruptible seed. A new bloodline. Adam as your natural father does not matter anymore. God as your Heavenly Father, and Jesus as the firstborn among many of the same brethren is what matters!

Romans 8:29 (AMP), *"For those whom He foreknew [of whom He was aware and loved beforehand], He also destined from the beginning [foreordaining them] to be molded into the image of His Son [and share inwardly His likeness], that He might become the firstborn among many brethren."* I like the Amplified here where it says, "molded into the image of His Son." This brings us to the picture of a potter and His clay. Isaiah 64:8 says, *"But now, O LORD, thou art our father; we are the clay, and thou our potter; and we all are the work of thy hand."* But the "not finished work" way of looking at this says, "He's molding us, and someday He's going to be finished with us. Someday we'll be conformed into His image. We'll get there... someday."

Friends, the molding happened on the cross! We are molded! Look at Romans 12:2, another verse that speaks of being conformed. *"And be not conformed to this world: but be ye transformed by the renewing of your mind, that ye may prove what is that good, and acceptable, and perfect will of God."* Think about this for a minute: If the Apostle Paul is warning us not to be conformed to this world, that means we are ALREADY transformed. If we were still in and of the world, we would already BE conformed to it. But the warning here is, "Don't go back to the world, but continue to transform yourself into what you've been transformed into by the renewing of your mind!" We are not conformed to this world but we HAVE BEEN transformed. And we're going to look at the renewing of our mind a lot later on.

Romans 8:29 (MSG), *"God knew what he was doing from the very beginning. He decided from the outset to shape the lives of those who love him along the same lines as the life of his Son. The Son stands first in the line of humanity he restored. We see the original and intended shape of our lives there in him."* This is a beautiful translation to me. We see the original and intended shape of our lives in Him. We see our EPIC destiny... in Him. And the more we see Him, the more His life BECOMES our life. That's not us BEING molded though. That's us figuring out what we look like now that we've BEEN molded!

A lot of what follows is going to be about the two seeds: Adam, or the carnal, corruptible seed, and Jesus, the heavenly, incorruptible seed. It's about who we really are and how we BE who we really are. We are not the seed of Adam, but the seed of Abraham. The seed of faith. Not the seed of Adam, but the seed of David. The seed of Kingly authority. We are not the seed of Adam. We are the seed of Jesus!

Chapter 1

Speaking of Jesus

Before we even get started with this thing I think it's important to do this chapter called, "Speaking of Jesus." Because it is vital that we understand that every word in every verse in every book of the Bible is... speaking of Jesus. It's all Him. The Old Testament looks forward to Jesus (while displaying Him in types and shadows). The Gospels show Him as He was, show His earthly ministry, and His sacrifice on the Cross. And the New Testament looks back at what He did and what it means. But it is ALL Jesus.

Jesus said, in John 5:39, *"Search the scriptures; for in them ye think ye have eternal life: and they are they which testify of me."* In the Message Bible it says, *"You have your heads in your Bibles constantly because you think you'll find eternal life there. But you miss the forest for the trees. These Scriptures are all about me!"*

This is important because we become what we behold. If we look at the Bible as a "how to live" manual then we are missing the point. We are focusing on what WE are doing, not on what Jesus DID. And, as we're going to see, when Jesus spoke He wasn't telling us how to behave, He was describing Himself. And He did this so that once He Himself took up residence in us we would have a better understanding of WHO was in us, and how HE operated.

Let me give you an example: The be-attitudes. "Attitudes we are supposed to be in." Well... hold on a second. Let's really look at it. And I'm not going to put the whole passage here, but I want to list the "attitudes we're supposed to be in." Ok. Poor in spirit. They that mourn. The meek. They that hunger and thirst after righteousness. The merciful. The pure in heart. The peacemakers. They which are persecuted for righteousness' sake.

Now traditional teaching would have us believe that Jesus was giving us a list of qualifications we need to have, or achieve. Basically we have been taught that Jesus was telling us what to do. He was putting a yoke on us and telling us how to behave. "Be poor in spirit. Mourn. Be meek. Etcetera."

But what Jesus was really doing... was describing Himself. Jesus is poor in spirit. Jesus mourned. Jesus is meek. Jesus hungered and thirsted after righteousness. Jesus is merciful. Jesus is pure in heart. Jesus was persecuted for righteousness' sake. He wasn't putting a yoke on us at all. He was, as always, talking about Himself.

Jesus came so that we could see what the Father looks like. He told Phillip, "If you've seen me you've seen the Father." Hebrews 1:3 says about Jesus, *"Who being the brightness of his glory, and the express image of his person, and upholding all things by the word of his power, when he had by himself purged our sins, sat down on the right hand of the Majesty on high."* Jesus is the express image of the Father, and the brightness of His glory.

But Jesus didn't show us what the Father looked like so that we could TRY to look like Him. He showed us what the Father looks like so that we could understand what, on this side of the cross, WE look like!

Another example of this is the "love chapter," 1 Corinthians 13. The Apostle Paul goes through a long list of what love is. Look at it in the Message Bible, *"Love never gives up. Love cares more for others than for self. Love doesn't want what it doesn't have. Love doesn't strut, Doesn't have a swelled head, Doesn't force itself on others, Isn't always "me first," Doesn't fly off the handle, Doesn't keep score of the sins of others, Doesn't revel when others grovel, Takes pleasure in the flowering of truth, Puts up with anything, Trusts God always, Always looks for the best, Never looks back, But keeps going to the end. Love never dies..."* (1 Corinthians 13:4-8).

And, again, we think these are things we have to do in order to love. We think we have to force ourselves to care for others more than ourselves in order to love. We think we have to stop wanting what we don't have in order to love. We think it's all about US, and what WE'RE doing.

But that's not it at all. Listen: God IS love. So when Paul is describing love... He's describing God. He's describing Jesus. Jesus never gives up. Jesus cares more for others than Himself. Jesus doesn't force Himself on others. Jesus doesn't keep score of sins.

It's all about Jesus. All of it. Every word in every chapter in every book of the Bible. All of these things that we think we're supposed to try to do... are really personality profiles of Jesus. Jesus showed us the Father. The Bible shows us Jesus. But not so we can try to be like Him. So we can know what we are really like!

Jesus is the light of the world. He shines in the darkness and makes the darkness flee. And we--in our human mindsets--always take this to mean that the darkness is bad so it has to go. But really all the darkness is, is the inability to see. You can't see when it's dark out. Which can be scary.

But according to 1 John 4:8, *"There is no fear in love; but perfect love casteth out fear: because fear hath torment. He that feareth is not made perfect in love."*

If you're afraid, it's because you can't see things the way they really are. And do you know what comes with that? Torment! But when you start to understand how much Daddy loves you... that'll drive out the fear. That'll drive out the darkness. And you'll be made perfect in the perfect love of the Father. And, of course, when I say you'll be "made" perfect, what I mean is that you'll be REVEALED perfect--not to God, but to yourself.

See, God doesn't test us so that HE can know what's in our heart. He already knows. He tests us so that WE can know what's in our hearts.

James 1:2-4, *"My brethren, count it all joy when you fall into divers temptations; Knowing this, that the trying of your faith worketh patience. But let patience have her perfect work, that ye may be perfect and entire, wanting nothing."*

Patience does a perfect work. And that perfect work is NOT perfecting us, but it is showing us what it means to BE perfect! You can't get any more perfect than having the Perfect One living inside you. The perfection part happened when you were conformed into His image on the cross.

But even though we're already at the finish line of the race, it's still a marathon. And we still need to see how we GOT to the finish line. We ARE conformed into His image, but we need patience in diverse temptations so that we don't get frustrated, but instead begin to see what His image is in real world situations!

Jesus is the answer to every problem. He is the Lord of all. His name is above every name, and He is the solution to all of life's trials. Listen, the Bible is not the revelation of things to come. It is not a "how to live" manual. It is, quite simply, the revelation of the Lord Jesus Christ. Everything in the Bible speaks of Jesus.

Why is this important? Because when we use it to try to impose standards on each other, or on ourselves, we are setting ourselves up for failure. Our EPIC destiny is not to try and fail. It is to BE who we are.

Look at the last part of James 5:16, *"...the effectual fervent prayer of a righteous man availeth much."* How we preach this is, "If you're righteous, and you pray fervently, then it'll avail much." But that's taking the emphasis off of Jesus and putting it on us. There's only ever been one truly righteous man. His name is Jesus.

The effectual fervent prayer... of Jesus... availeth much. The Bible isn't telling us what to do. It's telling us who Jesus is, what He did, and what it means for us.

Continuing with this thought: *"But this man, because he continueth ever, has an unchangeable priesthood. Wherefore he is also able to save them to the uttermost that come unto God by him, seeing he ever liveth to make intercession for them"* (Hebrews 7:24-25). Jesus is the righteous man whose prayer avails much. And Jesus ever lives to make intercession for us. Now THAT is some good news!

God doesn't hear anything except what Jesus says. That's why it's so important to understand that even when we pray for each other... it's not US praying. It's Jesus. Who is my intercessor? Jesus. Who is the mediator between God and man? The man Jesus.

This is why it's vital to completely identify with Jesus. This is why it can be frustrating when we take things into our own hands. We think if we pray super hard (or fervently) God will move. But what we don't understand is that God already moved! We don't need a move of God. We need a revelation of Jesus!

Praying in Jesus' name does not mean saying, "In Jesus name we pray, Amen." It means praying in Jesus' nature, or authority. Letting Jesus pray for us, and in us, and through us. Frankly, in light of the truth that we ARE Jesus, it's a little silly to say that at the end of a prayer. It'd be like me talking to someone and ending with the phrase, "In Thomas' name I speak, Amen." It's not when we SAY His name that power comes. It's when we SPEAK in His name. It's when we understand that HE is the one speaking in and through us.

I have another example of Jesus speaking of Himself, but I want to save it for the chapter on faith.

So I'll kind of wrap this one up with what I think I'm trying to say. We need to see Jesus everywhere. We need to see Him, first, in every word of every chapter of every book of the Bible. And then, when we start to see Him everywhere in history (HIS story) then we can start to see Him everywhere in our lives.

On the cross Jesus didn't just remake man. He remade the WORLD in His image. Matthew 19:28 in the Amplified Bible says it like this, *"Jesus said to them, Truly I say to you, in the new age [the Messianic rebirth of the world], when the Son of Man shall sit down on the throne of His glory, you who have [become My disciples, sided with My party and] followed Me will also sit on the twelve thrones and judge the twelve tribes of Israel."*

The world--everything--was reborn on the cross. Born from above. Everything was made new. We're going to explore all of this more later on, but Jesus created... A new heaven and a new earth. A New Day. A New Creation. A new seed. A new age. And look what Jesus said would happen in that new age: We sit on twelve thrones and judge the twelve tribes of Israel.

This means that we have been given Jesus' authority to make what's true in heaven... true on earth. We've been put in the position of judge of this new world. What we speak IN JESUS' NAME is what comes to pass. When we speak OF Jesus... and speak AS Jesus... we make true for us, and those around us, what was made true on the cross!

Now let's bring this home: Galatians 6:7-8, *"Be not deceived; God is not mocked: for whatsoever a man soweth, that shall he also reap. For he that soweth to his flesh shall of the flesh reap corruption; but he that soweth to the Spirit shall of the Spirit reap life everlasting."*

This passage goes right along with what we're going to see regarding the corruptible and incorruptible seed. Sowing and reaping. But... WHO is this passage talking about?

The fact of the matter is that you (or I) haven't reaped everything we've sown, either good or bad. And thank God for that. We've all done things in our life that could have--and should have--been a lot worse, if not for the mercy and grace of God. See, mercy is you not getting what you deserve, and grace is you getting what you don't deserve.

Galatians 6:7-8 is not talking about YOU sowing and reaping. It's talking about the only men that have ever lived. It's talking about Adam, who sowed to his flesh, or the human effort that is the tree of knowledge of good and evil, and reaped corruption. And it's talking about Jesus, who sowed to the Spirit and reaped life everlasting.

The Bible is talking about Jesus! Only when we find ourselves IN Jesus is the Bible talking about us. It's not a "how to live" manual. It's not a set of rules. It's a revelation of Jesus. When we see HIM clearly, we begin to see ourselves clearly.

Paul wasn't telling us to be careful about sowing and reaping... because we aren't the farmer! Jesus is the farmer, the Word is the seed, and we are the ground! We don't sow or reap. We bear fruit according to what has been planted in us.

Jesus is the vine and we are the branches. Jesus, the firstfruit, is holy, and that makes the rest of the lump holy. It's not about US sowing and reaping. It's not about OUR flesh, or human effort. It's not about what WE do. It's about what Jesus did.

Chapter 2

Incorruption

There are two dimensions in the universe that we live in: The world and the Kingdom. Earth and Heaven. Darkness and Light. The lie and the Truth. Adam and Jesus. Corruption and Incorruption. And here's what I want to say before we even get into the main passage of Scripture for this book: The truth is the truth whether you know it or not and whether you believe it or not. The key is that knowing it and believing it makes the truth true... for you. We want to walk in the fullness of who Jesus is and what Jesus did.

Ok.

1 Corinthians 15:42-53, *"So also is the resurrection of the dead. It is sown in corruption; it is raised in incorruption: It is sown in dishonour; it is raised in glory: it is sown in weakness; it is raised in power: It is sown a natural body; it is raised a spiritual body. There is a natural body, and there is a spiritual body. And so it is written, The first man Adam was made a living soul; the last Adam was made a quickening spirit. Howbeit that was not first which is spiritual, but that which is natural; and afterward that which is spiritual. The first man is of the earth, earthy: the second man is the Lord from heaven. As is the earthy, such are they also that are earthy: and as is the heavenly, such are they also that are heavenly. And as we have borne the image of the*

earthy, we shall also bear the image of the heavenly. Now this I say, brethren, that flesh and blood cannot inherit the kingdom of God; neither doth corruption inherit incorruption. Behold, I shew you a mystery; We shall not all sleep, but we shall all be changed, In a moment, in the twinkling of an eye, at the last trump: for the trumpet shall sound, and the dead shall be raised incorruptible, and we shall be changed. For this corruptible must put on incorruption, and this mortal must put on immortality."

Now before I go any further I have to explain something. In my "theology," I'm not waiting for anything to happen. I believe everything already happened on the cross. I believe the cross is the most important thing that has ever happened in the history of, well, history. I believe it is what the entire Old Testament looked forward to and what the entire New Testament looks back to. I believe the book of Revelation is not in our future, but in our past. The book of Revelation is an in-depth look at what happened on the cross! I don't believe the above passage is going to happen. I believe it already happened!

When Jesus said, "It is finished," that's exactly what He meant. We don't have to wait for anything. We simply have to apprehend what we've been apprehended of. We have to fight the good fight of faith and lay hold of eternal life! We have to figure out what Jesus did and what it means.

And what Jesus did is, He took our corruption onto Himself, sowed it in corruption with His death, and burial, and reaped it in incorruption with His resurrection! We bore the image of Adam before the cross. But on this side of the cross we bear the image of Jesus! The old man is dead and the New Man has come forth!

Let's unwrap some of this passage.

"So also is the resurrection of the dead." This is what we're talking about. We're not talking about making an old man behave. We're not talking about making bad people good. We're talking about making dead people alive! Because Jesus didn't come to improve you, He came to remove you!

John 11:25 says, *"Jesus said unto her, I am the resurrection, and the life: he that believeth in me, though he were dead, yet shall he live."*

Jesus didn't say, "I'm going to be the resurrection someday." He said, "I AM the resurrection." And then He literally raised dead Lazarus back to life. But He also said He IS the life. On the cross Jesus drew (or dragged) everybody into Himself. So when Jesus died, everybody died. And then, because He is the resurrection, when He rose back to life, everybody rose back up... to HIS life!

Life as we know it isn't good enough. Life as we know it is corruptible. It's dark and ugly. It's carnal and fleshly. Just like Adam. Adam, the first man, was a living soul. He was ruled by his mind, will, and emotions. He was lacking something--lacking the Holy Spirit. And because a seed can only produce after its own kind, Adam could only produce more living souls. He couldn't give us what we needed because he didn't have what we needed.

Enter Jesus. The first man Adam was a living soul. The last Adam (Jesus) is a quickening Spirit. He brought what we were lacking. He took His super and put it on our natural to bring us out of the world and into the supernatural Kingdom of God! The King has come, and Adam has left the building! Welcome to Graceland!

And look at this, Jesus had to come as God in the flesh, in order to be sown in corruption. He had to completely identify with us in order for us to be able to completely identify with Him. He became who we were so we could become who He is. In our passage above, in verse 44, it says, *"It is sown a natural body; it is raised a spiritual body."* The natural body had to die so the spiritual body could live.

Jesus said, *"Verily, verily, I say unto you, Except a corn of wheat fall into the ground and die, it abideth alone: but if it die, it bringeth forth much fruit"* (John 12:24).

18

This is why Jesus had to die. People mistakenly preach that Jesus died so we could live. That's not the case. He didn't have to die so we could live. He had to die so that we could die. And He had to rise again so that we could rise again. He had to rise again so that we could live. But not just so we could live "A" life. He rose again so that we can live HIS life! Or, more accurately, so Jesus can live His life in and through us. By dying, in and as Jesus, and rising again, in and as Jesus, we have been sown in our natural body, but raised into HIS Spiritual body!

Jesus brought what Adam was missing.

Now there are a lot of ways to preach the story of Adam, and original sin, but for our purposes we're going to look at it like this: Adam was a living soul, natural, corruptible. In Adam we were born into death. Born into the dimension of sin and death. James 1:15 says, *"Then when lust hath conceived, it bringeth forth sin: and sin, when it is finished, bringeth forth death."* This was Adam's problem. He lusted after the fruit of the tree of knowledge of good and evil.

Now let me qualify this. Eve, the woman, who represents the soul (or the mind, will, and emotions) was very much one flesh with her husband. They were two parts of the same being, so to speak. And look at Genesis 3:6, *"And when the woman saw that the tree was good for food, and that it was pleasant to the eyes, and a tree to be desired to make one wise, she took of the fruit thereof, and did eat, and gave also unto her husband with her; and he did eat."* God told Adam not to eat of the tree. But his woman, his soul, wanted to. That's human nature. That's what happens when you aren't led by the Spirit. If someone tells you not to do something, that's what you want to do. That's why God found fault with the Law, or the Old Covenant. Because it demanded perfection without being able to produce it.

Adam lusted after knowledge. He lusted after being, not only "like" God, but actually being God. The story of Lucifer (which I believe is the story of Adam) bears this out. Lucifer wanted to ascend into heaven and exalt his throne ABOVE the stars of God (Isaiah 14:13).

Adam was made in the image of God, but that wasn't enough for him. He wanted more.

His lust conceived original sin (which is, in my opinion, the only sin). It caused him to stop believing God. God said, "You don't have to do anything in order to receive from me." The serpent said, "You need to eat the fruit in order to be like God." And Adam believed the serpent. He should have told the serpent, "I don't have to do anything to be like God... I'm already like God." But he didn't. He took a stand and said, "My effort is what is going to make me righteous. Getting enough knowledge about right and wrong is going to allow me to stop acting wrong and start acting right."

Look at Deuteronomy 6:25, *"And it shall be our righteousness, if we observe to do all these commandments before the LORD our God, as he hath commanded us."* It will be OUR righteousness. Adam wanted to do it himself and have it for himself. He wanted to earn righteousness. But self-righteousness is no kind of righteousness at all.

2 Corinthians 5:21 says, *"For he hath made him to be sin for us, who knew no sin; that we might be made the righteousness of God in him."* The righteousness OF GOD in Him. Again, this is why Jesus had to come to earth as a human. He had to be born into corruption, just as we were, so that He (and we in Him) could be born again into incorruption! And He had to be sowed in the natural, so that He could rise again into the Spiritual.

That's what Adam was missing, and that's what Jesus brought: The Holy Spirit. And not just a visitation of the Holy Spirit, but a habitation! An indwelling of the Holy Spirit. This is what molds us--or, in fact, reveals to us the molding that happened on the cross. It's not an outward change, but an inward change!

Ephesians 4:21-24 (MSG), *"My assumption is that you have paid careful attention to him, been well instructed in the truth precisely as we have it in Jesus. Since, then, we do not have the excuse of ignorance, everything--and I do mean everything--connected with that old way of life has to go. It's rotten through and through. Get rid of it! And then take on an entirely new way of life--a God-fashioned life, a life renewed from the inside and working itself into your conduct as God accurately reproduces his character in you."*

This is where Adam missed it, where he couldn't do it. He didn't know Jesus. He tried to be God--in fact HIGHER than God--and instead of ascending he plunged the world, and humanity, into a cursed dimension of sin and death; a rotten, corruptible way of life. He thought that if he had enough information about good and evil, that information would allow him to live the life he lusted after.

But that was never what God wanted. That's why God told him not to eat of that tree. It's not about good and evil at all, it's about LIFE! It's about a God-fashioned life. A life renewed from the inside. It's about Jesus inside us working His way out as we realize that He HAS accurately reproduced His character in us. He HAS conformed us to His image. He HAS transformed us into a new creature. IT IS FINISHED!

The sowing happened on the cross. The much fruit came at the resurrection--that's you and me and everybody else. The corruptible seed died and the incorruptible seed come forth. That's what it means by "the twinkling of an eye." It happened in an instant 2,000 years ago. And, in a practical way, it happens in an instant in each of our lives in the waters of baptism. But we'll get to that.

The difference between the corruptible and incorruptible seeds is the Holy Spirit. And as we'll see, the seed is the heart. The Holy Spirit, or the circumcision of the heart (made without hands), is what makes the difference. The Holy Spirit is what changed (past tense, even though it feels like it is changing, present tense) everything.

Verse 43 of 1 Corinthians 15 says, *"It is sown in dishonour; it is raised in glory: it is sown in weakness; it is raised in power."* This is the difference between Jesus and Adam. This is the difference between the two seeds. Adam dishonored God and made everything corruptible. *"Wherefore, as by one man sin entered into the world, and death by sin;*

and so death passed upon all men, for that all have sinned" (Romans 5:12).

See, Adam brought sin--unbelief--into the world. And because he didn't believe God, and chose good and evil rather than life, he died. He was a walking dead man. And since he could only produce after his kind, all of humanity was the walking dead. Adam and Eve didn't have a child until AFTER they were cut off from the Tree of Life. All of humanity was born in the fallen dimension of the world--outside of the garden, or paradise, of God.

What it took to redeem humanity was the literal Tree of Life (Jesus) becoming us so we could become Him.

Romans 5:18 (MSG), *"Here it is in a nutshell: Just as one person did it wrong and got us in all this trouble with sin and death, another person did it right and got us out of it. But more than just getting us out of trouble, he got us into life!"*

Jesus took Six Steps to the Throne, both for us and as us. He did everything that was necessary to redeem us from the curse of sin and death that Adam plunged us into. He did everything that was necessary to reconcile us back to God. He did everything that was necessary in order to plunge us, not into sin and death, but into our EPIC destiny!

Jesus didn't just get us out of trouble. But think about that for a minute: If ALL Jesus did was get us out of trouble, that would have been WAY more than enough. But He didn't just get us out of trouble. He did more than that. He got us into life. And not just any life... but HIS Life! Eternal, abundant, everlasting, Resurrection Life.

The thing we seem to miss the most about this is that we try to live Jesus' life. We try to follow Jesus. We try to act the way He acted. But if you're acting like Jesus, then that's all it is: An act. If you're trying to follow Him, you will fail. Nobody can live Jesus' life... except Jesus. And the truth of the matter is, it's not us living at all. It's Jesus living His life in and through us!

Galatians 2:20 says, *"I am crucified with Christ: nevertheless I live, yet not I, but Christ liveth in me: and the life which I now live in the flesh I live by the faith of the Son of God, who loved me and gave himself for me."* We're going to look at this verse again when we talk about faith, but for now I want to focus on the, "Christ liveth in me," part.

Nothing can be more important than this revelation. It's not me that lives. I died once when I was born into Adam (before the cross) and I died again when I was crucified with Christ. The life God wanted me to have was impossible from the start because of what my natural father, Adam, did. So that "Adam life" of sin and death... had to die. That's what the second death is. The death of death. And that second death happened on the cross.

When we get to baptism we're going to see that it happens there too, in a sense, but for now we're talking big universal themes.

So I died when I was born into Adam, and then I died on the cross. Basically, I'm dead. No two ways around it. Which is what Jesus said in Luke 17:33, *"Whosoever shall seek to save his life shall lose it; and whosoever shall lose his life shall preserve it."* Either way, you lose your life. Because God doesn't want you to have YOUR life. He wants you to have HIS Life!

He doesn't want you to be corruptible. He wants you to be incorruptible. He doesn't want you to be the seed of Adam. He wants you to be the seed of Abraham and David! The incorruptible seed of the Lord Jesus Christ! He doesn't want you to endure (regular) life, He wants you to enjoy (Resurrection) Life!

Continuing with 1 Corinthians 15:43, *"...it is sown in weakness; it is raised in power."* Adam tried to sow in his power, but he quickly found out that he didn't have any. It's not OUR righteousness that matters. It's God's righteousness. It's not OUR power. It's His power. Jesus said, in 2 Corinthians 12:9, that, *"...My grace is sufficient for thee: for my strength is made perfect in weakness..."*

When we think we are strong, God will let us try to be strong. When we want to do things our way, He'll let us. He told Adam not to eat of the tree of knowledge of good and evil, but He didn't stop Adam. He gave Adam a measure of free will. I'm convinced that God is too much of a gentleman to force His will on us. Now, when He saved all of us on the cross, He didn't give us free will then. That's why I say a measure of free will. He lets us live how we want to. He lets us make decisions. And as long as we want to be in charge, He'll let us.

It's not until we are weak that He steps in to be strong. It's like when someone is drowning: You don't want to go try and help them right away, because they have a lot of fight in them and they might take you down with them. But when they stop fighting... then you can save them.

Jesus' strength is made perfect in our weakness. He became a servant. He became weak for us and as us so that we could become strong in Him and as Him. He sowed our weakness and raised His power!

This next part is my favorite part of the whole 1 Corinthians passage: Verse 49 says, *"And as we have borne the image of the earthy, we shall also bear the image of the heavenly."* This goes back to that measure of free will. We didn't have free will when we were born into Adam. And we didn't have free will when we were born into Jesus on the cross. We bore the image of Adam through no fault, or choice, of our own. And we now bear the image of Jesus through no effort, or choice, of our own.

Here's what I'm saying: Look in the mirror and Jesus looks back at you. He's in there (not in the mirror... in you!). You have already been conformed to His image. You're not of a corruptible seed, you're of an incorruptible seed. You bore the image of Adam because you didn't know who you really were.

In John 17:3 Jesus says, *"And this is life eternal, that they might know thee the only true God, and Jesus Christ, whom thou hast sent."*

It's not about GETTING anything. It's about knowing what we got on the cross. It's not about being conformed, it's about knowing that we've been transformed! Our EPIC destiny is not in our future, it's in our past!

When we know God, and His Son Jesus--and we know them through the Holy Spirit--then we "enter into" eternal life. We begin to live the abundant, everlasting life that we've been given by letting Jesus live His Life in and through us!

A seed can only produce after its own kind. An apple seed can only produce apples. Adam, a living soul, could only produce more living souls. Jesus, the Lord from heaven, can only produce... Jesus.

God has always had a plan for His people. For His seed. And this seed took two main forms: The Seed of Abraham, and the Seed of David. We'll take the next two chapters to look at each seed, and come to the conclusion that each seed is culminated in Christ!

Chapter 3

The Seed of Abraham

When I think about the seed I think about covenant. But I think we have a profound misunderstanding regarding even the word, "covenant." I'm going to get to Abraham, but first I think we need to look at covenant; what it really is, what it really means, what we think of it, and what God thinks of it.

The first time the word, "covenant" is used in the King James version of the Bible is in Genesis 6:7-8. God says to Noah, *"And, behold, I, even I, do bring a flood of waters upon the earth, to destroy all flesh, wherein is the breath of life, from under heaven; and every thing that is in the earth shall die. But with thee will I establish my covenant; and thou shalt come into the ark, thou, and thy sons, and thy wife, and thy sons' wives with thee."*

God said, "I'm going to destroy all flesh, wherein is the breath of life. I'm going to get rid of the wicked(ness) of the world. But because of the grace, Noah, that you found in my eyes, I'm going to put you in the ark and bring you out of the world and into the Kingdom."

The ark, of course, is Jesus. He is the vehicle, so to speak, of our salvation. When we were placed in Him, our corruptible seed (of wickedness and flesh) died. And a new incorruptible seed was planted. Our baptism was an underwater heart transplant! Our stony, stiffnecked heart was removed and God's fleshy, loving heart was inserted.

God's first--and really His only--covenant was, "I'm putting you in the ark." He put us in Jesus. And look what the word, "covenant" means: H1285, "in the sense of *cutting*. A *compact* (because made by passing between *pieces* of flesh)." God's covenant is the cutting away of our flesh. The circumcision of the heart.

And really, more than a heart transplant, what the circumcision made without hands did is it cut away the flesh around our heart, and revealed God's heart in our chest!

Deuteronomy 10:16 declares God's heart on the matter, *"Circumcise therefore the foreskin of your heart, and be no more stiffnecked."* Even under the Old Covenant economy, God was concerned with the heart, and not the flesh. He was concerned with our motives, not our actions. He was concerned with WHO WE ARE, not what we do. Because God knows that once we understand who we really are, what we do will flow naturally from that revelation.

See, circumcising our hearts is what ALLOWS us to be no more stiffnecked. It's not, "Circumcise your heart and try really really hard not to be stiffnecked." It's, "BY circumcising your heart you ARE no longer stiffnecked." In the Old Covenant God wrote His laws on tablets of stone. In the New Covenant He writes His new law (the perfect law of liberty) on the fleshly tables of our hearts. It's not an outward change, but an inward change. It's not following the ark, but getting INTO the ark, as the ark gets into us.

And, as always, the key is understanding that JESUS circumcised our hearts. We can't do it, and luckily for us we don't need to. Jesus did the circumcising. Jesus did the conforming. Jesus did it all. HE did the work. We simply enter into the Finished Work that Jesus did by believing that He did it.

Jesus, speaking of the Holy Spirit, said, *"I will not leave you comfortless: I will come to you. Yet a little while, and the world seeth me no more; but ye see me: because I live, ye shall live also. At that day ye shall know that I am in my Father, and ye in me, and I in you"* (John 14:18-20).

We're in Him because He's in us, and we're in the Father because He's in the Father, and the Holy Spirit is what ties it all together. That's the first covenant God made with man: We were put in the ark when the Holy Spirit (the ark, Jesus) was put in us! The Holy Spirit is the Comforter, the Spirit of Truth. The Holy Spirit is the heart of God in man. The Holy Spirit is the incorruptible seed that IS the Lord Jesus Christ!

And another interesting point: God said He was going to destroy everything "under heaven." But He didn't destroy Noah or his family, or the animals... that were in the ark. Which says to me that when you're in the ark (in Jesus) you aren't UNDER heaven... you're IN heaven! These are the days of heaven on earth. Heaven isn't only someplace we go when we die. Heaven is where we went when Jesus died! Heaven is where we are right now! Again, we're in heaven because heaven's in us. That was God's first covenant.

So. Abraham.

Genesis 17:1-7 says, *"And when Abram was ninety years old and nine, the LORD appeared to Abram, and said unto him, I am the Almighty God; walk before me, and be thou perfect. And I will make my covenant between me and thee, and will multiply thee exceedingly. And Abram fell on his face: and God talked with him, saying, As for me, behold, my covenant is with thee, and thou shalt be a father of many nations. Neither shall thy name any more be called Abram, but thy name shall be Abraham; for a father of many nations have I made thee. And I will make thee exceeding fruitful, and I will make nations of thee, and kings shall come out of thee. And I will establish my covenant between me and thee and thy seed after thee in their generations for an everlasting covenant, to be a God unto thee, and to thy seed after thee."*

Here's where it gets down to it: God made a covenant with Abraham AND HIS SEED. God said He would bless Abraham to be a father of many nations. That's why Abraham is known as the father of faith. It's through Abraham's seed--those that believe--that God's everlasting covenant is made manifest.

Three times in the New Testament the phrase, "Abraham believed God," appears: Romans 4:3, *"For what saith the scripture? Abraham believed God, and it was counted unto him for righteousness."*

Galatians 3:6, *"Even as Abraham believed God, and it was accounted to him for righteousness."*

James 2:23, *"And the scripture was fulfilled which saith, Abraham believed God, and it was imputed unto him for righteousness: and he was called the Friend of God."*

This is the key to the whole deal: You believe God, and you get everything that Abraham was promised. You believe God, and you are Abraham's seed. You believe God, and you become the righteousness of God (the Lord Jesus Christ). Abraham didn't do anything special in his life... except believe God. And that was more than enough.

What we need to understand is that it's not a natural seed, but a Spiritual one. Romans 4:13 says, *"For the promise, that he should be the heir of the world, was not to Abraham, or to his seed, through the law, but through the righteousness of faith."* The Law demands perfection, but can't produce it. The Law was step one in God's plan, but it was never the fullness of God's plan. The Law was given as the tutor to bring us to Christ. It was given so that all would be judged guilty so that God could have mercy on all.

Faith in Jesus is what makes us God's righteousness, and faith is what makes us Abraham's seed. It is what brings us into the New Covenant. We're going to talk a lot more about faith later on, but for now we need to understand that Abraham's faith is what God found acceptable. Period.

Look at Genesis 12:1-4, *"Now the LORD had said unto Abram, Get thee out of thy country, and from thy kindred, and from thy father's house, unto a land that I will shew thee: And I will make of thee a great nation, and I will bless thee, and make thy name great; and thou shalt be a blessing: And I will bless them that bless thee, and curse him that curseth thee: and in thee shall all families of the earth be blessed. So Abram departed, as the LORD had spoken unto him, and Lot went with him: and Abram was seventy and five years old when he departed out of Haran."*

God said, "Go," and Abraham went. It was this simple act of faith, of listening to God and doing what He said, that activated everything else.

But think about this a little bit: Abraham is 75 years old. He's already an old man. He doesn't have any children. And God says, "I will make of thee a great nation." Which I suppose is doable, if Abraham had a baby right then at the beginning of the journey. But he didn't. In fact, he doesn't conceive the promised child until he's 99 years old! That's 24 years of believing God. That's faith.

That's why Abraham is not only the father of a great nation, he's the father of faith. The first in the line of a new, incorruptible seed. A faith-based seed.

And I want to touch on this real quick too: God promised to bless Abraham. Somehow we've gotten it into our heads that as believers we are supposed to be poor. And if we have anything we are supposed to give it all away. We've somehow equated holiness to poverty. But this isn't what God says. This isn't His promise, or His covenant.

God promised to bless Abraham, but He also says, "...and thou shalt be a blessing" (Genesis 12:2). See, we are blessed... to be a blessing. It's ok to have stuff, but the problem comes when stuff has you. If you're greedy, you're missing the heartbeat of God. If you're greedy, the seed is not only corruptible, but corrupted.

I think a lot of this poverty-based mindset comes from Jesus telling someone to sell all they have a give it to the poor. But let's see what

Jesus ACTUALLY said to the rich young ruler, and let's see what He MEANT.

Luke 18:18-24, *"And a certain ruler asked him, saying, Good Master, what shall I do to inherit eternal life? And Jesus said unto him, Why callest thou me good? none is good, save one, that is, God. Thou knowest the commandments, Do not commit adultery, Do not kill, Do not steal, Do not bear false witness, Honour thy father and thy mother. And he said, All these have I kept from my youth up. Now when Jesus heard these things, he said unto him, Yet lackest thou one thing: sell all that thou hast, and distribute unto the poor, and thou shalt have treasure in heaven: and come, follow me. And when he heard this, he was very sorrowful: for he was very rich. And when Jesus saw that he was very sorrowful, he said, How hardly shall they that have riches enter into the kingdom of God!"*

There are a couple of problems with this rich young ruler. First off, he wanted to EARN his inheritance. An inheritance isn't earned, it is passed down from the father to the son (or the Father to the Son). Secondly, he was self-righteous enough to believe that he had kept the Ten Commandments. Now whether or not he really kept all of them or not, I can't say. Jesus didn't rebuke him, but if he HAD kept all of the commandments... under that economy... he would have been in line for the inheritance.

What I CAN say is what Jesus said. Jesus said, "you're lacking something." Even if his ACTIONS were right, his HEART wasn't right. He had stuff, he was very rich, but his problem was, his stuff had him. Jesus told him to be generous, and he couldn't do it. He went away very sorrowful. He had stored up treasures on earth, and he valued them more than the treasures in (and of) heaven.

This is the same warning that Jesus gave in Matthew 6:19-20, *"Lay not up for yourselves treasures upon earth, where moth and rust doth corrupt, and where thieves break through and steal: But lay up for yourselves treasures in heaven, where neither moth nor rust doth corrupt, and where thieves do not break through nor steal."*

Earthy riches are corruptible. They don't last. We don't even REALLY own them. God created, and owns, everything. So the key, once again, is to understand that God blesses us... to be a blessing.

When the people asked John the Baptist what they should do, this is what he said, *"He answereth and saith unto them, He that hath two coats, let him impart to him that hath none; and he that hath meat, let him do likewise."* John didn't say give away everything you have. He said if you've been blessed enough to have two coats, and you see someone without one... give them a coat. He says, "You were blessed, so be a blessing." Not, "God wants you to give away everything you have and be poor."

And this doesn't just apply to money. According to Ephesians 1:3 we have been blessed with all spiritual blessings in heavenly places in Christ. And, one of the more popular Biblical phrases when it comes to money, "Freely you have been given, freely give," actually says, *"Heal the sick, cleanse the lepers, raise the dead, cast out devils: freely you have received, freely give"* (Matthew 10:8). It has nothing to do with money.

But it does take us back to Abraham. God told Abraham, "Walk before me and be thou perfect"(Genesis 17:1). It was part of the command, part of the promise, and part of the covenant. Basically he told Abraham, "in order to be the first of this incorruptible seed, you can no longer be corruptible." But God wasn't giving Abraham mission impossible. He wasn't just telling Abraham TO be perfect, He was telling him HOW to be perfect.

By walking before God, literally, "Walking FACING God," Abraham was transformed into what he beheld. He received faith FROM God, so that he could have faith IN God. And he passed that faith on to his seed.

Adam, the natural father, could only produce after his kind. He disobeyed God and because of that lack of faith he produced sin and death. And that's what his offspring produced as well. Because it's all they COULD produce.

Abraham broke that cycle though. And when he produced the promised seed, it was an incorruptible seed. We're going to look at Abraham's supposed shortcut into Hagar's tent (and the corruptible seed that came from his human effort) a little bit later, but for now we want to look at Isaac, the promised son.

Genesis 17:19, *"And God said, Sarah thy wife shall bear thee a son indeed; and thou shalt call his name Isaac: and I will establish my covenant with him for an everlasting covenant, and with his seed after him."* For now what we need to understand about the seed of Abraham is that it wasn't about Abraham producing anything. It was about God producing something IN Abraham. It was about the covenant, and the promised seed.

Between Abraham and Sarah there was zero chance of producing a child. They were past the age of human effort making God's promise happen. It took faith. Hebrews 11:11-12 says, *"Through faith also Sara herself received strength to conceive seed, and was delivered of a child when she was past age, because she judged him faithful who had promised. Therefore sprang there even of one, and him as good as dead, so many as the stars of the sky in multitude, and as the sand which is by the sea shore innumerable."*

Abraham was as good as dead. Sarah was past the age of conceiving and delivering a child. Human effort plain straight was not going to get the job done. And, really, that was God's point. He didn't want anybody to be able to take credit for what HE was doing through those that had faith in Him.

Ephesians 2:8-9 bears this out: *"For by grace are ye saved through faith; and that not of yourselves: it is the gift of God: Not of works, lest any man should boast."*

If God promises something... GOD delivers on it. We don't have to make it happen, we simply have to believe that God will make it happen. That's why we have verses like, *"Except the LORD build the house, they labour in vain that build it"* (Psalm 127:1). Now don't misunderstand me, He builds in and through us, but only because of our faith. Our faith is the key that unlocks the door, and lets God move.

The seed of Abraham is incorruptible, because the seed of Abraham is Jesus. The covenant is an everlasting covenant because it's all about Jesus. It's HIM holding up both ends of the bargain. This is powerful to me, and I touch on it in *Identity Crisis*, but it bears repeating here.

In Abraham's day, when you made a covenant with someone, you literally cut covenant. You took an animal (or animals), and cut it in half, and the two people who were involved in the covenant passed between the animal together. Now this is so cool to me. Look at what happened when God cut covenant:

Genesis 15:17-18a, *"And it came to pass, that, when the sun went down, and it was dark, behold a smoking furnace, and a burning lamp that passed between those pieces. In the same day the LORD made a covenant with Abraham, saying, Unto thy seed have I given this land..."*

ABRAHAM NEVER PASSED BETWEEN THE ANIMALS!!!

Abraham was asleep. Which to me says that Abraham was in a posture of rest. None of his effort was involved in the covenant. God made covenant... with Himself... and He included Abraham in it because of Abraham's faith.

And He summed up the covenant by saying, "Unto thy seed have I given this land." The Promised Land. A land called rest. A land named Jesus. A land entered into, not through human effort, but through faith.

Jesus is the incorruptible seed, and Jesus is the land that was promised. As usual, in my "theology," it's all Jesus.

Galatians 3:26-29, *"For ye are all the children of God by faith in Christ Jesus. For as many of you as have been baptized into Christ have put on Christ. There is neither Jew nor Greek, there is neither bond nor free, there is neither male nor female: for ye are all one in Christ Jesus. And if ye be Christ's, then are ye Abraham's seed, and heirs according to the promise."*

There's so much here, and I promise we're going to unravel it, but I just wanted to qualify Jesus as Abraham's seed. When we believe in Jesus, (believe that we ARE Jesus) we are brought into the covenant the same way that Abraham was. And I say we must believe that we ARE Jesus, because HE is the seed.

Galatians 3:16, *"Now to Abraham and his seed were the promises made. He saith not, And to seeds, as of many; but as of one, And to thy seed, which is Christ."*

It's not seeds. It's seed. It's not a bunch of us. It's One. It's not Jews and Greeks. It's not male and female. It's not bond and free. It's Jesus. Period.

And more and more I'm coming to understand that it's only all of us coming into unity that WE make up Jesus. ALL of us. Believers AND unbelievers (which is what Paul meant when he said neither Jew nor Greek). Guys, I'm convinced that unbelievers are simply believers that don't know yet.

So since Jesus is the incorruptible seed, since it's His heart beating in our chests that transforms us into Him, and puts us in line for the Father's inheritance, I'm convinced that that's where our focus needs to be. We look to Abraham, but we see Jesus. We take example from Abraham's faith--believing and obeying God--but our faith is perfected in the Perfect One.

Even the story of Abraham and Isaac and the burnt offering is a direct parallel to God and Jesus and the cross. God told Abraham to sacrifice his only son; the son of promise. The incorruptible seed. And

Abraham was willing to do it. But more importantly, Isaac was willing to do it.

Isaac wasn't a little kid that Abraham could boss around. Isaac was obedient to his father. And in the same way Jesus was obedient to His Father. Abraham (or God, in this case) sacrificed his only son, Isaac (Jesus). And this part was always powerful to me too, in Genesis 22:2 when God is talking about Isaac He says, *"...take now thy son, thine only son Isaac, whom thou lovest..."* Isaac wasn't Abraham's only son...! Abraham had already produced Ishmael through human effort with his bondwoman! (More on this later, I promise.)

But in God's eyes, the corruptible seed didn't factor into the equation. The promise was to the incorruptible seed. The promise was not to Adam, but to Jesus. Not to the Old Man, but to the New Man. Not to Ishmael but to Isaac. Our EPIC destiny has nothing to do with the old, and everything to do with the new. Luke 3:38 identifies Adam as the son of God. But in John 3:16 Jesus identifies Himself as the only BEGOTTEN Son. See, Adam was God's son, just as Ishmael was Abraham's son, but Isaac was Abraham's only son, as Jesus is God's only Son!

Our EPIC destiny is to come into the fullness of who Jesus is. And who He is... in us. He IS the Promised Land of rest that God swore to give to Abraham and his seed. Which means WE are in the Promised Land because the Promised Land is in us. A land that flows with milk and honey (righteousness and revelation). A land that is, quite simply, the Kingdom of God. But the Kingdom has to have a King.

The covenant that God made with Abraham was that his seed should possess the Promised Land. It is an everlasting covenant, because the Seed of Abraham is the eternal One, the Lord Jesus Christ.

The covenant that God made with David was that his seed should always sit on the throne; that the seed of David would rule the Promised Land with kingly authority. It is also an everlasting covenant because, as we're about to see, the Lord Jesus Christ is also the Seed of David.

Chapter 4

The Seed of David

As we mentioned, our EPIC destiny--being conformed into the image of Christ--really happened 2,000 years ago on the cross when we were transformed into the incorruptible seed that IS Christ. But it was promised many years before that. It was promised to Abraham, and it was promised to David.

The Seed of Abraham would possess the land, and the Seed of David would rule the land.

2 Samuel 7:10-13 says, *"Moreover I will appoint a place for my people Israel, and will plant them, that they may dwell in a place of their own, and move no more; neither shall the children of wickedness afflict them any more, as beforetime, And as since the time that I commanded judges to be over my people Israel, and have caused thee to rest from all thine enemies. Also the LORD telleth thee that he will make thee an house. And when thy days be fulfilled, and thou shalt sleep with thy fathers, I will set up thy seed after thee, which shall proceed out of thy bowels, and I will establish his kingdom. He shall build an house for my name, and I will stablish the throne of his kingdom forever."*

A couple of things here: God gave us a place of our own. He gave a wandering people a home. My nickname when I was a kid was "Tumbleweed." I was always restless. I never felt settled. And it wasn't until I got into Jesus (when I realized that He had gotten into me) that I found where I belonged. Having a Heavenly Father, a true Husband, and brothers and sisters in Christ... having a FAMILY... is so important.

Way back in the garden of Eden God said that it is not good for man to be alone. We are social creatures, and connection with each other is vital. That's why it's so important, again, to understand that the promise is not for the seeds, but for the seed. It's is not for you or me, it's for us. We, all together, make up one New Man: The Lord Jesus Christ. As a many-membered body we are the culmination of God's promise. The culmination of the Seed.

Next we see that in the Promised Land (that is rest, or Jesus), "neither shall the children of wickedness afflict them any more, as beforetime." Here's my take on "wicked people." There are only two men who ever lived, Adam (wicked) and Jesus (righteous). The Promised Land--the Kingdom of God--is for Jesus, not Adam. That's why there's no wicked(ness) in it. And, as we're going to see, it takes the death of the Old Man for the New Man to arrive, or enter into, the Kingdom. On the cross God separated the goats (Adam) and the sheep (Jesus). He got rid of everything in you that wasn't Jesus. He filled you with Himself. Basically, God got your goat 2,000 years ago, so you don't have to worry about any of that.

Verse 11 goes on to say that the covenant God made with David caused rest from all the enemies. This is big, and important. Because the fullness of this happened on the cross. Jesus came, and fought the war to end all wars, and defeated every enemy that we could, or would, ever have.

Look at 1 Kings 5:2-5, *"And Solomon sent to Hiram, saying, Thou knowest how that David my father could not build an house unto the name of the LORD his God for the wars which were about him on every side, until the LORD put them under the soles of his feet. But now the LORD my God hath given me rest on every side, so that there is neither adversary nor evil occurrent. And, behold, I purpose to build an house unto the name of the LORD my God, as the LORD spake unto David my father, saying, Thy son, whom I will set upon thy throne in thy room, he shall build an house unto my name."*

Again, we need to understand that the promise, or covenant, was made to David's SEED. David purposed in his heart to build God a house, but God wouldn't let him, because David was a man of war. But because David did all the fighting, and set his son up in a position where there was no one left to fight, Solomon was able (in the natural) to fulfill the promise. Spiritually, this is exactly what Jesus did. He wiped out all adversaries and evil. According to 1 John 3:8, *"...For this purpose the Son of God was manifested, that he might destroy the works of the devil."*

Now give me a minute to take a different spin on the devil. In my last book, "Six Steps to the Throne," I may or may not have killed him. But let's stop looking at him as a "him," and start looking at "him" as "the accuser." Or, an accusing thought. An accusing mindset. The spirit of antichrist. Which would be anything that is against your true identity IN Christ, and AS Christ.

So. If Jesus destroyed the works of the accusing mindset, and He nailed the handwriting of ordinances that was against us to the cross (Colossians 2:14), taking away the POWER of the Law to accuse us... then here's my question: What are we fighting against?

David conquered all the enemies, which made his son, Solomon, more than a conqueror. Jesus spoiled principalities and powers, and was raised higher than every other name in existence, and we were in Him when He did it. He did it both for us and as us. Which makes us more than a conqueror, but also leaves us nothing left to conquer. Friends, Jesus didn't say the work of a believer was to fight things. He said the work of a believer is to... well... believe.

1 Timothy 6:12 says, *"Fight the good fight of faith, lay hold on eternal life, whereunto thou art also called, and hast professed a good profession before many witnesses."* If you feel like you absolutely,

positively HAVE to fight something... this is it. Fight the good fight of faith. Fight against unbelief. Lay hold on eternal life.

Don't fight the devil, believe that Jesus defeated the devil.

Don't fight the Old Man, believe that Jesus buried him in the watery grave of baptism.

Don't fight unbelievers, believe that Jesus saved them too, and tell them the good news!

Solomon didn't have to fight, because his father did it for him. Solomon was free to fulfill the covenant and build God a house. We don't have to fight because Jesus fought for us. And we are free to enjoy the fullness of the covenant. We are free to walk in our EPIC destiny!

But here's the really cool part: David and Solomon wanted to build God a house. But look at what it actually says in 2 Samuel 7:11, *"...Also the LORD telleth thee that he will make thee an house."* Not, "He will make a house for you." He will make YOU a house. This is powerful!

Jesus, the carpenter, isn't up in heaven building a mansion for you to live in on streets of gold. No, what He did was, on the cross He built YOU into a house for HIM to live in!

Isaiah 66:1 says, *"This saith the LORD, The heaven is my throne, and the earth is my footstool: where is the house that ye build unto me? and where is the place of my rest?"*

We seem to think that we can contain God in a building. In fact, I think this is the problem with a lot of churches out there. We're so concerned with our four walls that we miss the whole world outside of them that needs what we have... needs who we are! We seem to have forgotten that the church isn't where we go, the church is who we are!

Hebrews 3:6 (MSG Bible) answers the question posed in Isaiah 66:1, *"Christ as Son is in charge of the house. Now, if we can only keep a firm grip on this bold confidence, we're the house!"*

When God promised David that He would build HIM into a house... this covenant was fulfilled in Jesus. Jesus transformed us into a house for God to live in, in the form of the Holy Spirit. And in 2 Samuel 7:13 God makes it even more specific and awesome, *"He shall build an house for my name, and I will stablish the throne of his kingdom for ever."*

We're not just "a" house. We are the house of God. Paul says, *"Know ye not that ye are the temple of God, and that the Spirit of God dwelleth in you?"* Jesus lives in us, and He lives through us. This is what makes the house that we are, a house for the name of the Lord. God promised that He would establish the throne of His Kingdom forever... in us.

When Jesus first arrived on the scene He said, *"...Repent: for the kingdom of heaven is at hand."* He told people, "Change the way you think, because things are about to change. We're shifting from the world to the Kingdom." And He said this change was at hand, it was close, because He was on the way to the cross.

Luke 17:20-21, *"And when he was demanded of the Pharisees, when the kingdom of God should come, he answered them and said, The kingdom of God cometh not with observation: Neither shall they say, Lo here! or, lo there! for, behold, the kingdom of God is within you."*

The Pharisees were all about observing rules, and laws, and religious ceremonies. But Jesus was trying to tell them that the Kingdom has nothing to do with all of that nonsense. It's not about what you observe. It's about what's inside you. It's about WHO is inside you! Jesus said it's not about what you can see--not about what you do--but it's about who you are!

The Kingdom, as simple as it can get, is the realm where the King rules and reigns. It is where Jesus is Lord. And here's the truth of the matter: Jesus is either Lord of all, or not at all. Now let me explain; Even when we act like we're in charge... we're not. We can't be. Jesus remade the world in His image on the cross. What happens when we act like we're in charge is that we begin to live a lie. We begin to go against our new, incorruptible nature. This doesn't, however, make us "sinners." What it does is it makes us the righteousness of God in Christ that is doing something he (or she) shouldn't be doing.

Jesus IS Lord of all. That's not up for debate. What we need to do is follow Paul's advice in Romans 12:1, *"I beseech you therefore, brethren, by the mercies of God, that ye present your bodies a living sacrifice, holy, acceptable unto God, which is your reasonable service."* We need to let Jesus do what He wants to do in our bodies. Period. And look at how Paul describes this, "your REASONABLE service." Which, when you realize what an awesome King we serve, makes sense. God has our best interests at heart. It is His good pleasure to give us the Kingdom.

God wants the best for us, and that's why He put the best (Jesus) IN us!

But remember that no children of wickedness are allowed. The Kingdom is for Jesus, not Adam. This, again, is the good fight of faith. BELIEVING that Colossians 1:12-14 is true. *"Giving thanks unto the Father, which hath made us meet to be partakers of the inheritance of the saints in light: Who hath delivered us from the power of darkness, and hath translated us into the kingdom of his dear Son: In whom we have redemption through his blood for forgiveness of sins."*

Your sins were forgiven, and you were translated out of the power of darkness (out of the world) and into the Kingdom of God's dear Son, Jesus. This is the inheritance of the saints in light. This is the covenant that God made way back with Noah. We were put into the ark, and the ark was put into us!

We were made Kings and Priests because Jesus, the King Priest, lives in and through us! We are the Seed of Abraham, and we are the Seed of David, because Jesus is the Seed, and He was planted in us!

David was promised that his seed would rule and reign forever. *"I have made my covenant with my chosen, I have sworn unto David my servant, Thy seed will I establish for ever, and build up thy throne to all generations"* (Psalm 89:3-4).

This is where our authority to not only possess the Promised Land, but RULE the Promised Land comes from. Unfortunately, it seems as if we always think of authority as something negative. Power corrupts and absolute power corrupts absolutely. Right? Well... not when it comes to Jesus.

John 5:25-27, *"Verily, verily, I say unto you, The hour is coming, and now is, when the dead shall hear the voice of the Son of God: and they that hear shall live. For as the Father hath life in himself; so hath he given to the Son to have life in himself; And hath given him authority to execute judgment also, because he is the Son of man."*

We think of authority as something that is used (or abused) in order to enforce corrupt, or bad, judgment. But, guys, I'm telling you, when Jesus said the hour is coming, and now is, He was talking about the cross. And when Jesus was lifted up on the cross He drew (dragged) all men into Himself. So that the judgment that Jesus executed was the judgment that He received!

And listen, Jesus was made sin for us. He was judged guilty. He got the death sentence. And since we were in Him, we got it too. We didn't escape God's wrath, we were punished to the fullest extent of the Law's authority. The wages of sin is death, and those wages were paid on the cross. BUT the gift of God is eternal life.

The King couldn't be an everlasting, incorruptible seed unless He defeated ALL enemies. And that includes the last enemy, death. Jesus was so full of life--real, everlasting, abundant, Resurrection Life--that not even death could hold Him down!

Jesus took the place of every man, by wrapping every man up in Himself. 2 Corinthians 5:14-15 lays it out, *"For the love of Christ constraineth us; because we thus judge that if one died for all, then were all dead: And that he died for all, that they which live should not henceforth live unto themselves, but unto him which died for them, and rose again."* This is the shift. This is repentance. Changing our mindset from self-centered to Christ-centered. Realizing that He not only died for me, but He died AS me. Understanding that Adam can't get into the Kingdom, but that's ok because Adam is dead.

This is the judgment that our kingly David authority gives us, *"For as in Adam all die, even so in Christ shall all be made alive."* You're dead. But that's only step one. Because you died in Adam (the first death), and then you died on the cross (the second death), now you're not just alive, but Jesus lives in you!

(I believe this is true for everybody. But not everybody receives the gift they've been given. We appropriate this life, or activate it, through the waters of baptism, but I'm telling you... we'll get to that.)

Jesus is the Seed of David. He is the eternal King that sits on the Throne of a present and everlasting Kingdom of believers. Look at this beautiful description of the Kingdom: *"Of the increase of his government and peace there shall be no end, upon the throne of David, and upon his kingdom, to order it, and to establish it with judgment and with justice from henceforth even for ever. The zeal of the LORD of hosts will perform this."*

Judgment and justice. Again, we think of these terms in the negative. "People do bad stuff, so they deserve judgment and justice." But think about this: If you were already judged on the cross, and God poured His wrath out on Jesus (and you were in Jesus), and all of your sins--past, present and future--are forgiven... it wouldn't be justice for you to be judged again. What am I saying? I'm saying in the New Covenant we have absolutely nothing to fear from God. We can run TO Him instead of running from Him.

1 John 4:16-18 says, *"And we have known and believed the love that God hath to us. God is love; and he that dwelleth in love dwelleth in*

God, and God in him. Herein is our love made perfect, that we may have boldness in the day of judgment: because as he is, so are we in this world. There is no fear in love; but perfect love casteth out fear: because fear hath torment. He that feareth is not made perfect in love."

Our King is a good King. He, literally, is love. Remember when we said it was our reasonable service to present our bodies to Him as a living sacrifice? That's because He loves us. He can't do anything else. Our part, as believers, is to dwell in His love. To live in His love. To love His love.

This gives us boldness about the day of judgment, which I'm 100% convinced is in our past. We don't have to fear His judgment, we have to dwell in His love. Because His judgment... is that He loves us. He loves us so much that He died for us. And He loves us enough to not only come back to life for us, but to come back to life IN US!

The Kingdom's government and PEACE has no end. Peace because there are no enemies left, and peace because the judgment happened 2,000 years ago. And I always like to add this part: Since Jesus is the Lamb of God slain before the foundation of the world... the judgment happened before anything else ever happened. It simply came to its fullness on the cross.

See, Jesus was born of a woman, but really He has always been. And this is important. Look at John 8:56-58, *"Your father Abraham rejoiced to see my day: and he saw it, and was glad. Then said the Jews unto him, Thou are not yet fifty years old, and hast thou seen Abraham? Jesus said unto them, Verily, verily, I say unto you, Before Abraham was, I am."*

This was a big deal for Jesus to say for two reasons. 1) He was claiming that He was eternal. 2) By saying, "I am," He was claiming to be God. In the next verse they took up stones to cast at Him. This was, basically, the ultimate blasphemy... unless it was true.

John 1:1 states, *"In the beginning was the Word, and the Word was with God, and the Word was God."*

Why am I spending time on this? Because everlasting life doesn't start when you die. It has always been. It is everlasting. It started before anything started and it never ends.

Revelation 1:8, *"I am Alpha and Omega, the beginning and the ending, saith the Lord, which is, and which was, and which is to come, the Almighty."*

There was never a time when Jesus wasn't present, and active in our lives. Like we saw earlier, either He's the Lord of ALL, or He's not the Lord AT all. He's always been the Lord, the King, and He always will be.

Hebrews 7:1-3 describes Melchisedec, who I believe was a Christophany, or an appearance of Jesus in the Old Testament. *"For this Melchisedec, king of Salem, priest of the most high God, who met Abraham returning from the slaughter of the kings, and blessed him; To whom also Abraham gave a tenth part of all; first being by interpretation King of righteousness, and after that also King of Salem, which is, King of peace; Without father, without mother, without descent, having neither beginning of days, nor end of life; but made like unto the Son of God; abideth a priest continually."*

King Priest... King of righteousness and peace... neither beginning of days or end of life, because He IS the beginning and the end. An eternal King sitting on an everlasting Throne ministering to the houses (us) in His Kingdom; ministering a righteous judgment of mercy and grace for those who dwell in His love... those who fight the good fight of faith and lay hold of eternal life. The same life that He has, and the same life that He gave freely to us.

Look at Hebrews 7:24-25, *"But this man, because he continueth ever, hath an unchangeable priesthood. Wherefore he is also able to save them to the uttermost that come unto God by him, seeing he ever liveth to make intercession for them."*

Read it in the Message Bible, *"But Jesus' priesthood is permanent. He's there from now to eternity to save everyone who comes to God through him, always on the job to speak up for them."*

Jesus is interceding for us. He's speaking up for us. He's telling His Heavenly Father, "In order to see somebody, you have to look at me. Because I'm in them and they're in me." When God looks at you, He sees Jesus, and when He looks at Jesus He sees you. As He is, so are we in this world. Our judgment is not scary, and it's not in our future. It's in our past, and it was in our favor!

Jesus, the Seed of David, is not a servant trying to be a King. He is a King with a servant's heart. Jesus said He didn't come to be served, but to serve. We don't need to serve Him, or think of Him as a cruel taskmaster. He serves us and provides all of our need according to His riches in glory!

David is spoken of like this, *"And when he had removed him, he raised up unto them David to be their king; to whom also he gave testimony, and said, I have found David the son of Jesse, a man after mine own heart, which shall fulfil all my will"* (Acts 13:22).

David was a man after God's own heart, and his Seed fulfilled God's will. See, David didn't HAVE God's heart--he couldn't, under the economy that he lived in--but he wanted it. He was after it. He loved God as best he could. Or let me say it another way: God's heart was in David's chest, but it was covered with flesh--human effort--and it needed to be circumcised. David tried as best he could to "act like a Christian," but he fell short because only Jesus can live Jesus' life.

This love and obedience that David was after... this servant's heart... was fulfilled in Jesus. David did it as good as he could, and then Jesus did it perfectly. And now it is fulfilled in us because Jesus not only DID it... but He DOES it in and through us!

Abraham believed, and it was accounted to him for righteousness. Jesus obeyed, and it is accounted to us for authority. *"For as by one man's disobedience many were made sinners, so by the obedience of one shall many be made righteous"* (Romans 5:19).

The King Priest ministry of Melchisidec was fulfilled in Jesus. He is the King of righteousness and judgment. And now it is fulfilled in us because Jesus lives in us. 1 Corinthians 6:2-3 says, *"Do ye not know that the saints shall judge the world? and if the world shall be judged by you, are ye unworthy to judge the smallest matters? Know ye not the we shall judge angels? how much more the things that pertain to this life?"*

We not only possess the Promised Land, the Kingdom, but we rule the Kingdom with Jesus' Kingly authority. Ecclesiastes 8:4 tells us, *"Where the word of a king is, there is power."* What we say--which is what we believe--is what will manifest in our lives. This is the authority that we have in Christ. When we pray in Jesus' name, when we speak the Word of God (which is Jesus, which is love) we speak the Kingdom into existence.

See, we've been given the land as the inheritance of the saints. But we've also been given the responsibility to not only live in the Kingdom, but to export the Kingdom. In Luke 12:48 Jesus says, *"But he that knew not, and did commit things worthy of stripes, shall be beaten with few stripes. For unto whomsoever much is given, of him shall be much required: and to whom men have committed much, of him they will ask the more."*

We have a responsibility as the Incorruptible Seed. Our EPIC destiny isn't just about who we are. It's about what we DO with who we are. We have been given something precious and valuable. We have been given much. We have been given the light of the world. When we were in darkness, it was easy for God to let us kind of wander around. But now that we've seen the light--now that we ARE the light--we have a responsibility to let that light shine.

One of my favorite verses in the Bible is Matthew 5:14, *"Ye are the light of the world. A city that is set on a hill cannot be hid."* Another one is Isaiah 60:1, *"Arise, shine; for thy light is come, and the glory of the LORD is risen upon thee."*

These verses are a rallying cry. Inspiration to take what we've been given and start sharing it with the world. Shining the light in the darkness so that there won't BE any darkness. Expanding the Kingdom (which is ever-expanding) by using Kingdom currency (which is love)! Showing things as they really are after the Messianic rebirth of the world that happened on the cross!

THIS is our EPIC destiny! To take what we've been given and show it to the world. Not to be conformed to the image, per se, because that happened on the cross. But to realize what the image IS that we have been conformed into, and to show that image to the world! The Kingdom has come, but it comes every time the Word is made flesh... every time Jesus does something in our bodies.

We're waiting for a second coming when the Lord will appear, but He's waiting to appear... in us! 1 John 3:2 in the Amplified Bible says, *"Beloved, we are [even here and] now God's children; it is not yet disclosed (made clear) what we shall be [hereafter], but we know that when He comes and is manifested, we shall [as God's children] resemble and be like Him, for we shall see Him just as He [really] is."*

And this verse isn't as confusing, or as futuristic, as it seems. See, we are already conformed to His image. We are already, even here and now, God's Son. So instead of waiting for Him to appear, instead of waiting for Him to conform us into His image, we need to see Him as He is. He has already appeared in us through the Holy Spirit. As He is... so are we in this world. We don't need Him to appear, we need to see Him as He really is. And when we see Him as He really is... we will BE Him as He really is!

The culmination of the Seed of Abraham, and the Seed of David, is the Kingdom of God's love ruling and reigning over every person in this world, and every inch of this world! Light shining in and on every man, woman, child, and situation so that there IS no darkness... no evil or adversaries occurant.

But just so we're clear, I'm still not putting a yoke on you. I'm not saying, "You've been given the light, you better let it shine." Because that's not the way it works. The way it works is that when we realize how full of light we are, we realize that we couldn't keep it from shining if we tried! It's not about DOING anything, not even shining the light. It's about seeing Jesus as He is, and letting Him BE who He is in us. It's about resting. It's about believing. It's about Jesus.

Chapter 5

Baptism

We now need to look at God's way of sealing the two covenants. He used circumcision to seal the covenant He made with Abraham, and He used the oil of anointing to seal the covenant He made with David. Both of these sealings happen in water baptism.

Genesis 17:7-11, *"And I will establish my covenant between me and thee and thy seed after thee in their generations for an everlasting covenant, to be a God unto thee, and to thy seed after thee. And I will give unto thee, and to thy seed after thee, the land wherein thou art a stranger, all the land of Canaan, for an everlasting possession; and I will be their God. And God said unto Abraham, Thou shalt keep my covenant therefore, thou, and thy seeds after thee in their generations. This is my covenant, which ye shall keep, between me and you and thy seed after thee; Every man child among you shall be circumcised. And ye shall circumcise the flesh of your foreskin; and it shall be a token of the covenant betwixt me and you."*

Remember earlier that we looked at the truth that God made a covenant with Himself and included Abraham in it. It wasn't up to Abraham to keep his half of the covenant. God said, "Possess the land that I give you." He gave it, and He empowers us to possess it. Abraham's part, our part, is to be circumcised. To circumcise the flesh of our foreskin.

"Circumcise" is number 4135 in Strong's Hebrew concordance and it means, "to cut short, blunt, or destroy." "Flesh" is H1320 and it means, "flesh, mankind, nakedness, self, or skin." Foreskin is the feminine version of H6188 which means, "exposed, or uncircumcised person." So what God told Abraham to do is to cut away the nakedness of the exposed person.

In the garden of Eden Adam and Eve were naked and not ashamed. It wasn't until they ate of the tree of death, the tree of knowledge of good and evil, that their nakedness bothered them. And what did Adam do about his nakedness? He tried to HIDE his nakedness. God doesn't want, or need for us to hide our nakedness from Him. He wasn't bothered by it. It wasn't a problem until ADAM'S eyes were opened to good and evil and then ADAM was bothered by it. What God wants is for us to destroy that entire mindset.

I don't want to be too graphic with this, but another way to look at this is to understand that the foreskin is the flesh that gets involved when the male member is planting his seed. It represents human effort. It's what happened when Abraham slipped into Hagar's tent and tried to produce the seed of promise with his own human strength.

This human effort HAS to be destroyed because God is not interested in what humanity can do by ourselves. God is interested in what HE can do in and through humanity.

Look at what Hebrews 11:12 says about Abraham, *"Therefore sprang there even of one, and him as good as dead, so many as the stars of the sky in multitude, and as the sand which is by the sea shore innumerable."* Abraham was as good as dead when he produced the promised child. It had nothing whatsoever to do with his human effort, because at that point he didn't have any human effort to use. He was circumcised. His flesh was cut away. The seed that came forth was no longer corrupted by his foreskin, it was simply the incorruptible seed of the Spirit.

And look at this in Deuteronomy 10:16, *"Circumcise therefore the foreskin of your heart, and be no more stiffnecked."* Which, of course, sounds like a command. Which, of course, we take right into the realm of the flesh (or human effort) and say, "I have to circumcise the foreskin of my heart so that I can be no more stiffnecked." We put the emphasis on ourselves. What we have to do.

But a few chapters later, in Deuteronomy 30 verse 6, the Bible says, *"And the LORD thy God will circumcise thine heart, and the heart of thy seed, to love the LORD thy God with all thine heart, and with all thy soul, that thou mayest live."* So we see that it's not US that does the circumcising at all. It's God who circumcises us. It's God who, really, overwhelms us with His love so that we can--out of the abundance of HIS love--love Him and love one another. Because when you're dealing with the heart, you're dealing with love. In fact, when you're dealing with God, you're dealing with love. Period. It's 100% all about love. But more on that later.

Before we move on to the anointing I want to point out that God told Abraham that this covenant is an EVERLASTING covenant. In verse 7 of Genesis 17 God says it is an, "everlasting covenant." And in verse 8 He says it is an, "everlasting possession." Why is this important? Because it means that no matter what you do you can't get kicked out of the Promised Land.

When it comes to who gets kicked out, Exodus 33:1-2 puts it like this, *"And the LORD said unto Moses, Depart, and go up hence, thou and the people which thou hast brought up out of the land of Egypt, unto the land which I sware unto Abraham, to Isaac, and Jacob, saying, Unto thy seed will I give it: And I will send an angel before thee; and I will drive out the Canaanite, the Amorite, and the Hittite, and the Perizzite, the Hivite, and the Jebusite."*

Two things here. First of all, the covenant God made with Abraham continued on to the people of Israel led by Moses. It's about the seed. The covenant stays in the seed. And secondly, the angel of the Lord went before them into the land to drive out the wicked (or, again, the wickedness) of the people who were there first. The Promised Land isn't for Adam. It's for Jesus. Adam, the corruptible seed, had to be driven out by Jesus, the incorruptible Seed, in order for Jesus (or us) to possess the land forever. And this driving out happened on the cross.

In our own lives this driving out happens in the waters of baptism. But I want to keep pointing out that I'm not talking about what happens when (if) we die. I'm talking about what happens when we're alive. I don't believe you have to be baptized to "go to heaven when you die." I believe you have to be baptized in order to live in heaven while you're alive!

Baptism is our death, so to speak, and our rebirth. It is how we enter into the covenant. It is how we identify with the sowing that Jesus did on the cross, and the reaping that Jesus did in His resurrection. It is how we make His death our death and His life our life.

But before we really talk about baptism we first need to look at the other sealing of the other covenant. The oil of anointing that was poured on David to mark and empower him to be king. And what's really interesting is that David was anointed three times. We'll look at all three but first I want to show the principal that God uses regarding the number three.

The number three stands for that which is solid, real, substantial, complete, and entire. It is the number of excellent things. Here are just a few examples:

2 Corinthians 1:10, *"Who delivered us from so great a death, and doth deliver: in whom we trust that he will yet deliver us."*

The "three tenses of salvation." Or, as I see it, the progression of salvation. And that's really important for us as we look at the anointing oil. Because it's a progression. But the most important part of the progression is to understand that we start the race with the race already being won. We aren't trying to finish the race. It is finished. The progression is simply finding out how the work got done, and what it means now that it is done.

1 Corinthians 13:13, *"And now abideth faith, hope, charity, these three; but the greatest of these is charity."*

See, in a manner of speaking, it starts with faith, moves on to hope, and culminates in love. It's a progression. But at the same time, faith is not just the starting point. It is what activates everything, but it also IS everything.

John 14:6, *"Jesus saith unto him, I am the way, the truth, and the life: no man cometh unto the Father, but by me."*

We start on the way, move through the truth, and into the life. It's a progression. It's a journey--not to get anywhere--but to understand where we are. It's a journey into the heart of how things really are. And how things really are is the heart of God.

Romans 8:30, *"Moreover whom he did predestinate, them he also called: and whom he called, them he also justified: and whom he justified, them he also glorified."*

Our EPIC destiny, being predestinated to be conformed into the image of Jesus, is found in this three-fold progression. We are called, justified, and glorified. But, again, we're not BEING conformed. Our Eternal Purpose In Christ was made manifest on the cross. It's not about being conformed. It's about finding out what it means that we HAVE BEEN conformed.

And Mark 4:8, *"And other fell on good ground, and did yield fruit that sprang up and increased; and brought forth, some thirty, and some sixty, and some an hundred."*

This is the progression. And I've heard it preached like this: Thirty is 30% God and 70% you--you've received the Lord, but you still consider yourself to be mostly in control. Sixty is 60% God and 40% you--more and more the will of Lord is being found in your life as you submit to Him more and more. An hundred is 100% God and 0% you-- you know who you are and you know it's not you at all, it's all Him.

It's important to point out too, that Jesus said SOME thirty, SOME sixty, and SOME an hundred. I'm convinced that you can be as close to God as you realize you are. See, we have been given 100%. It's available to us. But I don't believe God will force His will on us. I believe He wants us to apprehend what we've been apprehended of. If we're ok with 30, then that's what it is. Same with sixty. But if we want 100... it's ours for the taking.

So there's a progression. There's learning and growing. There's grace to grow (but that's another chapter). There are three anointings.

1 Samuel 16:13, *"Then Samuel took the horn of oil, and anointed him in the midst of his brethren: and the Spirit of the LORD came upon David from that day forward. So Samuel rose up and went to Ramah."* The first time David was anointed to be king he was anointed among his brethren. This is the 30. This is where it started. And look, right from the beginning the Holy Spirit came upon David. And it stayed with him from that day forward. That's what's so important about the anointing! It's the oil of anointing that represents the Holy Spirit!

2 Samuel 2:4, *"And the men of Judah came, and there they anointed David king over the house of Judah. And they told David, saying, That the men of Jabeshgilead were they that buried Saul."* The second anointing. David is anointed King over the house, or the tribe, or Judah. It's bigger now. First his brethren, then one of the twelve tribes. Even though from the first anointing, David had the right to be king over all, he still had to grow into maturity.

And he had to wait until the first king was dead and buried. Saul, or Adam, reigned until he died. Saul died in battle. Adam died on the cross. Then David was anointed. Then Jesus began to rule and reign. The first (Adam) became last and the last (Jesus) became first.

2 Samuel 5:3, *"So all the elders of Israel came to the king to Hebron; and king David made a league with them in Hebron before the LORD: and they anointed David king over Israel."* The third and final anointing. King over all of Israel. The fulfillment of what was started with the first anointing. The culmination of the promise.

Abraham was given the promise, but had to wait until he was done trying to make the promise happen before he could receive it. He had to trust God to deliver on it. David was given the promise, but had to wait until he came to maturity. He had to grow into the knowledge of what it meant to be king.

This, at its essence, is the Christian walk: Resting in God and letting Him lead us into all truth. The truth of who He is, which is the truth of who we are. Because as long as we try to do it ourselves, as long as we don't understand what it means to be who we are, it's always going to be a struggle. And God doesn't want us to struggle. He wants us to enjoy the fruit of HIS labor!

Circumcision and anointing. It culminates in water baptism.

Matthew 3:13-17 in the Message Bible describes Jesus' water baptism like this, *"Jesus then appeared, arriving at the Jordan River from Galilee. He wanted John to baptize him. John objected, "I'm the one who needs to be baptized, not you!" But Jesus insisted. "Do it. God's work, putting things right all these centuries, is coming together right now in this baptism." So John did it. The moment Jesus came up out of the baptismal waters, the skies opened up and he saw God's Spirit--it looked like a dove--descending and landing on him. And along with the Spirit, a voice: "This is my Son, chosen and marked by my love, delight of my life."*

In the King James Bible Jesus tells John that He needs to be baptized in order, *"...to fulfill all righteousness."* And what that means is, God putting things right. God making us right with Him, but more importantly, allowing us to RECEIVE that we are right with Him. When Jesus was baptized He literally identified 100% with humanity. He

BECAME Adam. He became sin. And then when He died, Adam died. All died. So that when He rose again... no more Adam. Only Jesus.

When Jesus was baptized the Holy Spirit descended on Him. This is what happened to David when he was anointed with the oil. And this is so important because the Holy Spirit is our love receptor. It is what allows us to receive God's love.

Remember how Abraham had two sons, but God referred to Isaac as Abraham's only son? And remember how God had two sons--Adam and Jesus--but Jesus is God's only begotten Son? The difference between Isaac and Ishmael is that Isaac was the son of promise. Isaac was the incorruptible seed.

And the difference between Jesus and Adam is the Holy Spirit. Adam didn't know who he was. He didn't know God loved him. He was missing that love receptor. He was missing the Holy Spirit.

Jesus is God's beloved Son because Jesus allowed Himself to "be loved" by God. He had the Holy Spirit that allowed Him to receive God's love, and to be empowered by God's love. As soon as the Holy Spirit rested on Jesus, God declared that He loved Him. Because at that moment God's love had found a place where it could be received.

God loves everybody unconditionally. He IS love. There's nothing else that He can do. But the problem has never been God loving us. It's always been us not being able to receive it. It's always been us feeling unworthy, or feeling like we need to earn God's love. This is what baptism does: It unlocks God's Holy Spirit--the Spirit of love--that's inside of us so that we can begin to receive the love of the Father. In a very real way water baptism transforms us into the beloved Son of God!

But hear me on this: Baptism, or the cross that proceeded it, does NOT turn us into something that God can love. He already loved us. What it does is turn us into something that can RECEIVE God's love.

Circumcision and anointing is all righteousness being fulfilled. But I think it's important to say this here: I don't believe baptism has anything to do with salvation. I'm convinced that salvation--at least in the sense of "where we go when we die"--was accomplished on the cross. And I don't think it's something we should focus on, or worry about. Jesus never said, "I have come to save you from hell." He said, "I am come that you might have life, and have it more abundantly."

What baptism does is it unlocks what's inside you. The Holy Spirit is activated as the old man dies--when you enter the water--and the New Man comes forth--when you are raised out of the water! Water baptism is like the ticket into the Kingdom, if you can hear it that way. But, again, I believe we're all already there. It's not about GETTING THERE. It's about living where we are. It's about the end of wandering around like strangers in the land of promise, and it's about enjoying the milk and honey that flows in the Promised Land that is the Lord Jesus Christ!

Colossians 2:9-15, *"For in him dwelleth all the fulness of the Godhead bodily. And ye are complete in him, which is the head of all principality and power: In whom also ye are circumcised with the circumcision made without hands, in putting off the body of sins of the flesh by the circumcision of Christ: Buried with him in baptism, wherein also ye are risen with him through the faith of the operation of God, who hath raised him from the dead. And you, being dead in your sins and the uncircumcision of your flesh, hath he quickened together with him, having forgiven you all trespasses; Blotting out the handwriting of ordinances that was against us, which was contrary to us, and took it out of the way, nailing it to his cross; And having spoiled principalities and powers, he made a shew of them openly, triumphing over them in it."*

Baptism is the circumcision made without hands. Circumcision of the heart. Not just actions, but motives. This is interesting though, because when Jesus was baptized He didn't need to be circumcised. His heart was already perfect.

So what's the deal? Why did Jesus have to do it? He told John that it was in order to fulfill all righteousness. But He was already righteous. He was already perfect and spotless and sinless.

Well, as we're going to see in-depth next chapter, Jesus did it because we couldn't. He did it to MAKE us complete in Him. And complete doesn't mean someone who doesn't make mistakes. Complete means, "not lacking anything." And what was Adam lacking? The Holy Spirit! Jesus was baptized, and the Holy Spirit rested on Him. God gave the love receptor to Jesus, and then God gave Jesus to us!

Jesus is the firstborn among many brethren. And really, what this means is that Jesus came first and made us all... Him. Not sons with a little "s," but the beloved Son! God doesn't want a big family, so to speak. He just wants us to understand that we are His Son!

See, we were circumcised IN HIM (according to Colossians 2:11). It's not OUR circumcision that matters. It's His. It's not OUR anointing that matters. It's His. It's not OUR baptism that matters. It's His. Our baptism is our way of identifying with HIS baptism.

2 Timothy 2:12 says, *"If we suffer, we shall also reign with him: if we deny him, he also will deny us."* But I want to tell you that this verse means, "If we identify with His suffering, we can reign in and through Him. But if we don't... we can't." It doesn't mean you need to suffer. Jesus did the suffering on the cross. It means we are buried with Him in baptism, and are risen with Him into Resurrection Life!

Jesus was baptized in the Jordan river. When we are baptized, it's our way of suffering with Him. Our way of identifying with Him. But when Jesus was baptized in the Jordan river... it was HIS way of identifying with US!

Baptism is more than just an outward expression of an inward change. It's the unlocking of the inward change! It's how we put off the body of the sins of the flesh. It's how we put off the old man and put on the New Man. It's how we make what's true... true for us.

It's how we enter into life. It's how we enter into rest. It's how we activate the gift of the Holy Spirit that we were given!

We were dead in our trespasses in sins. And this doesn't just mean that, "because we sinned, we had to die." It means that BY sinning, we WERE dead! Sin, or unbelief, is what separates you from God. It's what disqualifies you from life, so to speak, and keeps you in the bondage of the dimension of death. Living death. Adam was the walking dead.

So what baptism does--what Jesus did on the cross--is the killing of the body of sin, and the bringing forth of the body of Christ! We were dead in our sins and the uncircumcision of our flesh. But God has quickened us together with Him. Jesus drew us all into Himself when He was lifted up from the earth on the cross. Then, when He died, we all died. And when He rose again, we all rose again!

God forgave all our trespasses, bringing us out of death and into life! And He didn't just forgive them, He took them away and forgot about them! Justified isn't, "Just as if I'd never sinned." Justified is, "In God's eyes I've never sinned, because Jesus never sinned and now I'm Jesus." We went from sinner to saint in the waters of baptism. The sinner died. The saint came forth.

Now, understand I'm not saying we--the Old Man--have never sinned. I'm simply saying the Old Man that sinned is dead and gone. So we--the New Man, Jesus--have never sinned. There was a transformation on the cross. A sinner saved by grace isn't a sinner anymore. Jesus took away the sin of the world. It's gone. It's not an issue anymore.

And just in case that's not enough, Jesus blotted out the handwriting of ordinances that was against us. This is the Law. The Ten Commandments. God wrote the Ten Commandments with His finger. That's what the handwriting is. And they were nailed to the cross. The enemy, the accuser, had the strength of the Law on his side... until the cross. You couldn't measure up to the standard of the Law. It demanded perfection, but couldn't produce perfection. All it could produce was guilt and condemnation.

Look at the difference between the Old Covenant and the New Covenant: *"The Government of Death, its constitution chiseled on stone tablets, had a dazzling inaugural. Moses' face as he delivered the tablets was so bright that day (even though it would fade soon enough) that the people of Israel could no more look right at him than stare into the sun. How much more dazzling, then, the Government of the Living Spirit? If the Government of Condemnation was impressive, how about this Government of Affirmation?"* (2 Corinthians 3:7-9 MSG).

Old Covenant: Government of Death and Condemnation. New Covenant: Government of Living Spirit and Affirmation.

Jesus moved us out of the dimension of sin, death, and condemnation and into the dimension of the life, Spirit, and the affirmation of the Father. And He did it by giving us an underwater heart transplant. By circumcising not just the foreskin of our seed producing member, but by circumcising the foreskin of our hearts!

Deuteronomy 30:6 says it like this, *"And the LORD thy God will circumcise thine heart, and the heart of thy seed, to love the LORD thy God with all thine heart, and with all thy soul, that thou mayest live."*

A couple of keys here: It was Jesus that circumcised us. We didn't do it. The cross did it. And, again, it was the heart that needed to be circumcised. The flesh (or human effort, trying to keep the Law) had to be cut away. Trying to do it ourselves never works. Especially when we understand it's not about our actions, it's about our heart. Or, more accurately, about getting rid of our heart and getting God's heart. It's about what we BELIEVE, not what we DO. Because what we believe dictates what we do.

1 John 4:19 says, *"We love him, because he first loved us."* This is so important. God gave us the Holy Spirit--His heart--so that we could RECEIVE His love. And by receiving it, we are empowered to release it. Release God's love back to God, and to each other. Release God's love back to God BY releasing it to each other!

See, it's not just about being conformed to the image of Christ. It's about living out that image. It's about receiving what we've been given...

and releasing it. We are not empowered to receive God's love just so that we can be happy because God loves us. It's more than that. We have been empowered to receive God's love SO THAT we can love! This is the image that we have been conformed into. The image of love working in and through a body.

Chapter 6

New Heaven and New Earth part 1

We have been transformed. We are a New Creation in Christ. Old things have passed away. The Old Man--Adam--died on the cross. We are no longer of the corruptible seed. We, in Jesus, were sown in corruption and raised in incorruption! We have a New Heaven and a New Earth.

This chapter will look at the New Heaven, and the next chapter will look at the New Earth.

Revelation 21:1, *"And I saw a new heaven and a new earth: for the first heaven and the first earth were passed away; and there was no more sea."*

The new heaven is our new mind; the mind of Christ. And the new earth is our new body; the body of Christ. In the Bible the sea represents the wicked, or wickedness. So how appropriate that when the first heaven and first earth--Adam--passed away on the cross, the result is that there is no more sea! No more wickedness! Everything was reborn and remade in the image of Jesus.

Let's start with the Old Heaven. The Old Man. The unregenerated, or reprobate mind. Let's look at what passed away so that we can really see what came forth.

Romans 1:28-32, *"And even as they did not like to retain God in their knowledge, God gave them over to a reprobate mind, to do those things which are not convenient; Being filled with all unrighteousness, fornication, wickedness, covetousness, maliciousness; full of envy, murder, debate, deceit, malignity; whisperers, Backbiters, haters of God, despiteful, proud, boasters, inventors of evil things, disobedient to parents, Without understanding, covenantbreakers, without natural affection, implacable, unmerciful: Who knowing the judgment of God, that they which commit such things are worthy of death, not only do the same, but have pleasure in them that do them."*

Whew! Sounds like some people you know right? WRONG! This is a picture of the Old Heaven. This is a picture of EVERYBODY before the cross. This is not a picture of people today, it is a picture of Adam. Remember that there are only two men who have ever lived: The first Adam, and the last Adam (Jesus). So instead of thinking that some people have an Old Heaven and some people have a New Heaven, what we need to see is that the Old Heaven passed away when Jesus died on the cross.

The man described in the above passage was a covenant breaker. That's why God had to make the covenant with Himself, and include us in it through our faith. He got rid of the reprobate mind on the cross and gave us the mind of Christ! He gave us access to Him by His Son. Jesus, the New Heaven, is what allows us to have faith in the first place (more on that in the faith chapter).

The man described in the passage above was worthy of death. Which we always take to mean, "If someone is acting like this... he's worthy of death. If someone is sinning, well, the wages of sin is death." But let's remember that the whole Bible is speaking of Jesus. Even the verses that we like to throw at each other.

Romans 6:23, for example, makes it pretty clear, right? *"For the wages of sin is death..."* Cut and dried, right? Well, first of all, those wages applied to Adam, and to Jesus. Adam sinned, and on the day he did so he died. Then Jesus BECAME sin, and on that day He died too. We were in Adam for the first death, and we were in Jesus for the second death. So, again, it's not about what YOU do, it's about what

Jesus DID. And that's not even the end of the verse in Romans. *"For the wages of sin is death; but the gift of God is eternal life through Jesus Christ our Lord."*

Death is not the end of the story. In fact, in a very real way, it is only the beginning. The second death is what allows the new birth. The death of the Old Man allows the birth of the New Man. Jesus sowed in corruption so He could reap in incorruption.

Death died and made way for life!

It's not about getting what we deserve. Not in the New Covenant. Not with a New Heaven and a New Earth. Not with a New Mind and a New Body. No, on this side of the cross it's about mercy and grace. Mercy is us NOT getting what we deserve, and grace is us getting what we DON'T deserve!

Another example of a verse we want to throw at each other is Hebrews 9:27, *"And as it is appointed unto men once to die, but after this the judgment."* As if to say, "Well, we're all going to die and then get judged, so we better behave ourselves while we're here or else." Sigh. The Bible is not about what we are supposed to do. It's about what Jesus did.

Hebrews 9:27-28, *"And as it is appointed unto men once to die, but after this the judgment: So Christ was once offered to bear the sins of many; and unto them that look for him shall he appear the second time without sin unto salvation."*

These verses are about Jesus. It was appointed to man ONCE to die. Jesus kept this appointment on the cross. And He kept it not only FOR us, but AS us. We died when Jesus died. We rose again when Jesus rose again. Our Heaven and Earth passed away and His Heaven and Earth came down out of heaven from God! The key, as always, is seeing Jesus as He is so that we can BE Him as He is. We find ourselves in Jesus, and we find Jesus in us. That's the connection, and the unity, and the covenant, that allows us to live the abundant, eternal, everlasting, Resurrection Life... by letting Jesus live His life in and through us!

Now this can be kind of tricky though, especially when it comes to talking about a new mind, because it doesn't always feel like we have a new mind. Old thoughts seem to stick around. Old mindsets, and old ways of doing things... old habits... can be hard to break. Sometimes we see somebody acting like Adam, and sometimes we catch OURSELVES acting like him!

But that's why Romans 12:2 is so important, *"And be not conformed to this world: but be ye transformed by the renewing of your mind, that ye may prove what is that good, and acceptable, and perfect, will of God."*

See, it's all about apprehending what we've been apprehended of. It's all about being transformed into what we've already BEEN transformed into! It's all about making what's true... true for us.

And it comes from the renewing of our mind. The word, "renewing," is number 342 in Strong's Greek Concordance and it means, "renovation." Old thoughts creep up on us and they need to be renovated. That's what 2 Corinthians 10:5 is talking about, *"Casting down imaginations, and every high thing that exalteth itself against the knowledge of God, and bringing into captivity every thought to the obedience of Christ."*

But here's the key: It's not about chasing thoughts. Because if you're focusing on the bad thoughts, that's what's going to define your reality. What you believe is what is real to you. What you magnify is what manifests in your life. It's not about condemning yourself for having a bad thought. It's simply about, "Oh, that thought wasn't from God, I'm going to let that one go." Just let it go.

Hebrews 12:1 says, *"Wherefore seeing we also are compassed about with so great a cloud of witnesses, let us lay aside every weight, and the sin which doth so easily beset us, and let us run with patience the race that is set before us."*

Sin, or unbelief, or any thought that exalts itself against the knowledge of God, can only beset us if we let it. But it's easy to let it. It's easy to trip and fall if we are focused on our own human effort. It is impossible to live the Christian life on our own. Only Jesus can live Jesus' life. And that's the point. We must renew our minds, and focus only on Him, in order to be transformed into Him... in order to let Him live His life in us and through us.

So how do we do this? By letting the mind of Christ--the New Heaven--that's already in us... BE in us.

I touch on this in Six Steps to the Throne, but it's a powerful truth, and a progression that we need to understand.

Isaiah 55:8-9, *"For my thoughts are not your thoughts, neither are your ways my ways, saith the LORD. For as the heavens are higher than the earth, so are my ways higher than your ways, and my thoughts than your thoughts."*

First things first: God said this under the Old Testament, Old Covenant economy. That's how things were... before the cross. But the cross changed everything. The cross got rid of the Old Heaven and the Old Earth. The cross got rid of the sea. The cross got rid of the separation between God and man by putting God IN man!

Now follow the progression: God's thoughts and ways--His mind, His heaven--were not our ways. So our ways, our thoughts, the old heaven, had to pass away. This is what the cross accomplished. The body of sin died so that the body of Christ could live.

Heaven was higher than the earth. But in Jesus, heaven and earth met. In Jesus, *"Mercy and truth are met together; righteousness and peace have kissed each other"* (Psalm 85:10). Jesus is the perfect hybrid of God and man. The Son of man, 100% human, and the Son of God,

100% divine. He is what brought everything together and got rid of any separation.

1 Corinthians 2:14-16 shows the progression, *"But the natural man receiveth not the things of the Spirit of God: for they are foolishness unto him: neither can he know them, because they are spiritually discerned. But he that is spiritual judgeth all things, yet he himself is judged of no man. For who hath known the mind of the Lord, that he may instruct him? But we have the mind of Christ."*

The first man, Adam, was of the earth and he was earthy. He was the natural man. He had a reprobate mind. He couldn't receive the things of the Spirit. He wanted to earn God's love, because without the Holy Spirit he couldn't receive it. Without the mind of Christ, Adam didn't (and couldn't) understand God's ways or God's thoughts.

See, we think God's ways are good and ours are evil. But good and evil are fruit of the same tree--the tree of death. God's ways (or I should say WAY because He only has one way, and that's Jesus) is love. Jesus is the WAY, the truth, and the life. This is the mind of Christ: understanding that every thought God thinks is love.

We think God is mad at us. But that's the mind of Adam, the mind of the world. Way back in the garden of Eden Adam thought that because of his sin--his unbelief that caused him to eat of the wrong tree-- God was mad and was going to punish him. But that's not what God said. God never said, "If you eat from the tree of knowledge of good and evil I'm going to get mad and punish you."

God said, *"But of the tree of the knowledge of good and evil, thou shalt not eat of it: for in the day that thou eatest thereof thou shalt surely die"* (Genesis 2:17). Basically God said, "I don't want you to eat from that tree, because the only thing it can produce is death." And God didn't want Adam to die. God loved (and still loves) Adam.

And think about this for a minute: It was the tree of KNOWLEDGE of good and evil. It was a tree of thoughts and ways.

Adam chose HIS way and HIS thoughts rather than simply feasting on the fruit of the Tree of Life. And the fruit of the Tree of Life--God's ways and thoughts--is love!

The thoughts of God are not, "I'm mad at you if you mess up." Jeremiah 29:11 spells out the thoughts of God, *"For I know the thoughts that I think toward you, saith the LORD, thoughts of peace, and not of evil, to give you an expected end."*

God doesn't think in terms of good and evil. That's man's thoughts. God's thoughts are so much higher than that. God thinks in terms of love, and an expected end. So what is this expected end? Our EPIC destiny! To be conformed into the image of Jesus! And, as we've seen, this expected end happened 2,000 years ago!

And I say 2,000 years ago, but really it happened before anything else happened. The Lamb was slain from the foundation of the world. Your destiny has never been in jeopardy. Before there was ever a sinner, there was a savior. Jesus is not plan B. He's plan A. He's THE plan.

Isaiah 46:9-10 says, *"Remember the former things of old: for I am God, and there is none else; I am God, and there is none like me, Declaring the end from the beginning, and from ancient times the things that are not yet done, saying, my counsel shall stand, and I will do all my pleasure."*

The former things of old... is the cross. Whether it was 2,000 years ago--in its fullness--or before the foundation of the world--in its timelessness--the most important thing that has ever, or will ever, happen is when God became man and died on a cross. At that moment He not only declared the end from the beginning, and spoke of things not yet done... but He finished it. He finished the work. He conformed you into His image. That was His counsel, and His pleasure.

"Yet it pleased the LORD to bruise him; he hath put him to grief: when thou shalt make his soul an offering for sin, he shall see his seed, he shall prolong his days, and the pleasure of the LORD shall prosper in

his hand" (Isaiah 53:10). It pleased God to bruise (which actually means, "beat to pieces, break, crush, destroy, humble, oppress, or smite) His Son so that He could make us all His Son. So that we could be reborn from an incorruptible seed. The corn of wheat had to die in order to bring forth a great harvest.

Look at Isaiah 53:10 in the Message Bible, *"Still, it's what GOD had in mind all along, to crush him with pain. The plan was that he give himself as an offering for sin so that he'd see life come from it--life, life, and more life. And GOD's plan will deeply prosper through him."*

This is the joy that was set before Jesus that empowered Him to endure the cross. This is the joy of the Lord that is our strength. This is God's way and His thoughts.

So the question becomes, "For who hath known the mind of the Lord, that he may instruct him?" And the answer is, "But we have the mind of Christ."

He gave us His mind on the cross. The Old Heaven passed away and the New Heaven came down from God out of heaven. The Holy Spirit didn't just come UPON us though. It was planted IN us. And that's the next part of the progression. Letting what's in us... BE in us.

Philippians 2:1-11, *"If there be therefore any consolation in Christ, if any comfort of love, if any fellowship of the Spirit, if any bowels and mercies, Fulfil ye my joy, that ye be likeminded, having the same love, being of one accord, of one mind. Let nothing be done through strife or vainglory, but in lowliness of mind let each esteem other better than themselves. Look not every man on his own things, but every man also on the things of others. Let this mind be in you, which was also in Christ Jesus: Who, being in the form of God, thought it not robbery to be equal with God: But made himself of no reputation, and took upon him the form of a servant, and was made in the likeness of men: And being found in fashion as a man, he humbled himself, and became obedient unto death, even the death of the cross. Wherefore God also hath highly exalted him, and given him a name which is above every name: That at the name of Jesus every knee should bow, of things in heaven, and things in earth, and things under the earth; And that every tongue should confess that Jesus Christ is Lord, to the glory of God the Father."*

This passage shows us what the mind of Christ is, and what the mind of Christ accomplished. The mind of Christ is the Holy Spirit. It is the Spirit of love. It is God's heart beating in our chests. It is what connects us and unifies us and transforms us into one many-membered body.

This is how the whole, "every knee shall bow and every tongue confess" part works. When we let this mind of Christ that's in us... BE in us... then we will bow and confess that Jesus Christ is Lord. See, it's not about Jesus forcing anything on anybody. It's about His love transforming us into that same love!

So that's the New Heaven: the mind of Christ. And according to Matthew 6:10 the Kingdom comes when God's will is done in earth as it is in heaven. So we need to talk about the New Earth. The new body. The body of Christ.

Chapter 7

New Heaven and New Earth part 2

The New Heaven is our new mind; the mind of Christ. The New Earth is our new body; the body of Christ. And when Jesus prayed, *"Thy kingdom come. Thy will be done in earth as it is in heaven"* (Matthew 6:10), He was talking about the manifestation of the Kingdom, but He was also talking about the divine order of the citizens of the Kingdom.

See, we have a new body--Jesus' Resurrection Body--but we are also PART of His body. There's a corporate aspect, and an individual aspect to the New Earth. But both ways, corporately and individually, the body comes in line with the mind. In earth as it is in heaven. It flows down from the top.

So there are two different ways to teach about the New Body. First we'll address the individual body. YOUR new body. Because make no mistake, your body has been transformed. When Jesus was sown in corruption, you were sown with Him. And when Jesus was raised in incorruption, you were raised with Him.

Romans 6:5 says, *"For if we have been planted together in the likeness of his death, we shall be also in the likeness of his resurrection."* Remember that it's not OUR sowing and reaping that matters. It is Jesus' sowing and reaping that matters. He became us and sowed our corruption so that we could reap His incorruption and become Him!

Here's what I'm trying to say: Jesus didn't ever get sick. He couldn't. He lives out of the Resurrection Life that is the love of God. He had an incorruptible body that flowed from the knowledge of His incorruptible mind. The head leads the body. What you believe defines your reality. And Jesus believed He couldn't get sick. In fact, He didn't believe in sickness or death at all. He knew what was true. He knew how it was (and is) in heaven. And He brought that to earth.

Now, before you start to say I'm talking about "mind over matter," or positive mental assent... I'm not. You can't just think happy thoughts and expect everything to work out. You can't believe you're a millionaire and start spending like crazy. That's not what we're saying. Because see, God doesn't want, "mind over matter." He wants HIS mind in the matter! He wants His thoughts to be our thoughts. That's why He gave them to us.

And sickness is not one of God's thoughts. In fact, in Exodus 23:25 God says, *"And ye shall serve the LORD your God, and he shall bless thy bread, and thy water; and I will take sickness away from the midst of thee."*

So when we serve God, by believing God, and when we get on the right diet--bread from heaven and living water--we will find ourselves full of life. And where there is life, there is no death. Where there is light, there is no darkness.

One of my favorite examples of how Jesus dealt with sickness is the man with the withered hand. This story will preach on a lot of levels--the hand representing the five-fold ministry, and the controversy about the sabbath--but for our purposes I want to look at it "in the natural."

Mark 3:1-5, *"And he entered again into the synagogue; and there was a man there which had a withered hand. And they watched him, whether he would heal him on the sabbath day; that they might accuse him. And he saith unto the man which had the withered hand, Stand forth. And he saith unto them, Is it lawful to do good on the sabbath days, or to do evil? to save life, or to kill? But they held their peace. And when he had looked round about on them with anger, being grieved for the hardness of their hearts, he saith unto the man, Stretch forth thine hand. And he stretched it out: and his hand was restored whole as the other."*

Again, there is a lot going on in this story, but I want to focus on Jesus' attitude about the sickness itself. He didn't get worked up about it. He didn't fast and pray and beg God for healing. He simply told the man to stretch out His hand. Jesus didn't see something sick. He saw what really was. And what He needed to do was simply shine His light on the situation so that everyone else could see things as they really were.

I can hear Jesus saying, "Stretch out your hand. There's nothing wrong with it. Your reprobate, unregenerated mind only THINKS there's something wrong. But I have come to set things right. I have come to declare the Kingdom. I have come to save that which is lost. I have come to give you my mind and my body. To give you life, and that more abundant."

The mind of Christ defines the body of Christ. There's no sickness in Jesus, so there can't be any sickness in us. Period. In earth as it is in heaven. We are defined by the voice of truth, by the Word of God. We are who God says we are. We are healed, and happy, and whole! We don't need to float around on a glory cloud because we ARE the glory cloud!

Proverbs 17:22 gives this key to our New Earth, *"A merry heart doeth good like a medicine..."* See, it's about the heart--or the mind--affecting the body. When our heart, or our New Heaven, is right, then our body, or our New Earth, will line up in divine order.

Jesus paid for our healing on the cross. Isaiah 53:5 says, *"But he was wounded for our transgressions, he was bruised for our iniquities: the chastisement of our peace was upon him; and with his stripes we are healed."* Jesus' suffering is what unlocks our abundant life. Peter picks this up in 1 Peter 2:24, *"Who his own self bare our sins in his own body on the tree, that we, being dead to sins, should live unto righteousness: by whose stripes ye were healed."*

Isaiah, before the cross, promises that by His stripes we will be healed. Then Peter, after the cross, tells us that by His stripes we WERE healed.

Friends... we don't need to be healed. We are healed. What we need is to see how we GOT healed. We don't need to be delivered. We are delivered. What we need is to see how we got delivered. We need to let our New Heaven affect our New Earth. We need the mind of Christ to reveal the truth of who we really are, so we can BE who we really are!

And I like how Peter connects our healing to the forgiveness, and the taking away, and the forgetting about our sins. Because I believe the biggest reason we don't see "healings," is that we have disqualified people by convincing them that they are sinners. We even tell people that God won't hear a sinner's prayer. And I guess technically maybe that's right. So that makes the key telling people that they AREN'T sinners! Telling people what Jesus did and what it means will not only qualify people, but it will empower people!

The effective, fervent prayer of a righteous man availeth much. And that righteous man is Jesus. And that righteous man is in you. And you're in Him. And He IS you and you ARE Him. So if there were any sinners left, maybe God wouldn't hear their prayers...

But as I was writing that, God sent me to Luke 23:42 where the thief (a sinner), who I believe is Adam, prayed to Jesus. *"And he said unto Jesus, Lord, remember me when thou comest into thy kingdom."* And rather than ignoring him, and rejecting him, and saying, "Sorry, you made your bed now you have to lie in it," verse 43 says, *"And Jesus said unto him, Verily I say unto thee, To day shalt thou be with me in paradise."* Jesus did what He always did: He gave grace and truth.

Jesus can't get sick, and He can't die. It is appointed to man ONCE to die. And Jesus kept that appointment both for us and as us on the cross. Jesus has an incorruptible body. And since we have been transformed into Him... we have been given this same incorruptible body. The physical aspect flows from the knowledge of Him. Knowing that He paid the ultimate price--He literally died--so that we could die. And then He rose again so that we could rise again.

The other aspect of the New Body, or the New Earth, is the corporate body. Ephesians 5:30 lays it out, *"For we are members of his body, of his flesh, and of his bones."* Basically, we're all on the same team. It's not about theological differences, or denominational differences. It's about Jesus. It's all about Jesus.

Ephesians 4:4 tells us that not only are we members of His body, but, *"There is one body, and one Spirit, even as ye are called in one hope of your calling."*

So not only are we members of His body... but His is the only body that exists. See, there are only two men that have ever lived: Adam and Jesus. They both died on the cross. ONLY Jesus rose again. That means, on this side of the cross, there is only one man. The New Man. Jesus. No longer are there sheep and goats. God got your goat 2,000 years ago. No longer are there saints and sinners. The sinner was saved by grace, and transformed into a saint.

When the Old Heaven and the Old Earth passed away, so did the sea--so did the wickedness of the world. Remember all of those mindsets and behaviors that were associated with the Old Earth? They are gone; Washed away in the flood of water baptism.

But here, again, is the question: If this is true, why doesn't it LOOK like it's true. If this is true, why do saints still act like ain'ts? Why do we still do things that we ought not to do?

Because God won't force His will on us.

He wants what's best for us, and He has equipped and empowered us to enjoy our EPIC destiny, but He still gives us a measure of free will. He is waiting for us to let the mind of Christ that's in us... be in us. He put it in there, but we have to use it. And when we do, everything else will line up.

See, Jesus didn't just heal us... He made us whole. He didn't make us a better version of ourselves, or Adam. Jesus made us... Jesus. He didn't just fix the physical part, He fixed the mental part too. He didn't just redeem our bodies, He gave us HIS body. He made us a part of His body. He didn't just bring us back to life, He brought us into HIS Life!

We can't talk about a many-membered body without talking about the members of that body. Listen, I am the body of Christ. So are you. But in another way I am PART of the body of Christ, and so are you. And while different members, we are equal members.

Romans 12:3-5, *"For I say, through the grace given unto me, to every man that is among you, not to think of himself more highly than he ought to think; but to think soberly, according as God hath dealt to every man the measure of faith. For as we have many members in one body, and all members have not the same office: So we, being many, are one body in Christ, and every one members of one another."*

Many members. One body. We are all connected. This is what Paul was talking about when he said, *"For no man ever yet hateth his own flesh; but nourish and cherisheth it, even as the Lord the church: For we are members of his body, of his flesh, and of his bones"* (Ephesians 5:29-30). We don't hate one another. That's the same thing as hating ourselves. Instead we esteem each other higher than ourselves. We nourish and cherish each other. We let God's love for US become our love for each other.

Each member has a function. We all have the same EPIC destiny (to be conformed into the image of Christ) but this manifests itself in many different ways. We are all called to the same calling--to love--but we all love in different ways.

1 Corinthians 12:12-19, *"For as the body is one, and hath many members, and all the members of that one body, being many, are one body: so also is Christ. For by one Spirit are we all baptized into one body, whether we be Jews or Gentiles, whether we be bond or free; and have been all made to drink into one Spirit. For the body is not one*

member, but many. If the foot shall say, Because I am not the hand, I am not of the body; is it therefore not of the body? And if the ear shall say, Because I am not the eye, I am not of the body; is it therefore not of the body? If the whole body were an eye, where were the hearing? If the whole were hearing, where were the smelling? But now hath God set the members every one of them in the body, as it hath pleased him. And if they were all one member, where were the body?"

You are uniquely positioned to touch people. And you are uniquely positioned to touch people in unique ways. Being part of the body of Christ, literally being Jesus, doesn't mean you lose who you are. It simply means you USE who you are for the Lord. I'm a writer. God didn't take that gift away from me when I began to come into relationship with Him. Instead, He took what He had given me (the talent and desire to write) and used it to touch people for His glory.

You don't have to give up anything to "be a Christian." God made you specifically... you. If you can dance, dance for the Lord. If you can play music, play music for the Lord. Whatever it is that's in your heart to do... do that! Don't think, "I can't preach, so God can't use me." Different people need to receive love in different ways. That's why the body has so many members. Don't try to be someone else. Just let Jesus be Himself in you!

God set the members in His body as it pleases Him. This means... you are where you are for a reason. My knee and my shoulder are both members of my body. But it would be uncomfortable for them to touch each other. You don't have to force things. You don't have to "push" Jesus on people. Sometimes you think you can't reach someone, or that you aren't making a difference, but there are a lot of members in this body. If you do your part, then that's all you can do.

1 Corinthians 3:6-8, *"I have planted, Apollos watered; but God gave the increase. So then neither is he that planteth any thing, neither he that watereth; but God that giveth the increase. Now he that planteth and he that watereth are one: and every man shall receive his own reward according to his own labour."*

79

See, I don't have to do it all. I do my part, you do your part, and since we're the same body, it all gets done. We are one. We are all in this together. I may reach people differently than you do, but it's really God reaching people THROUGH us. So, again, don't get so caught up on what YOU'RE doing and instead focus on what Jesus did, and what Jesus is doing in and through you!

Look at what happened when Jesus died, *"And the veil of the temple was rent in twain from the top to the bottom"* (Mark 15:38). The veil in the temple is what kept people out of the presence of God. And when Jesus died He got rid of this separation.

The veil was rent from top to bottom. This is important. This happened to show that it was God doing the rending, because if man tore the veil they would have had to tear it from bottom to top. But God doesn't want man to ascend up to Him. He sent His Son to come down to us!

The rending from top to bottom also happened because it starts with heaven and flows down to earth. It starts with the head and flows down to the body.

Isaiah 52:7 says, *"How beautiful upon the mountains are the feet of him that bringeth good tidings, that publisheth peace; that bringeth good tidings of good, that publisheth salvation; that saith unto Zion, Thy God reigneth!"* This is so important because it's one thing to HAVE the mind of Christ, but it's something else entirely to USE what we have. It's one thing to be given a gift, but it's something else entirely to RECEIVE it. Eternal life, the gift of God, has to get into our head, and then out through our feet.

We have to not only RECEIVE Jesus... but we have to RELEASE Him. We have to not only BE the light, but also SHINE the light. And listen, I'm not telling you to try really hard to shine your light. Because that's works and labor and works don't work. I'm telling you that when you begin to understand how full of light you are... you won't be able to keep yourself from shining! You will be a city on a hill. And a city on a hill cannot be hid!

Revelation 1:13 says, *"And in the midst of the seven candlesticks one like unto the Son of man, clothed with a garment down to the foot, and girt about the paps with a golden girdle."* Jesus was clothed with a garment down to the foot. It started at the head and flowed all the way down the body. It started with the New Heaven and clothed the entire New Earth!

Our thinking, or our mindset, or our believing, WILL affect our actions, or our behavior. Bottom line: You do what you believe. You don't do what you SAY you believe, or what you WANT to believe. Your beliefs dictate your behavior.

Wrong believing produces death. Believing that your hand is withered will cause you to act like you have a withered hand. Believing that you are a sinner will cause you to sin.

But right believing produces life. Right believing produces right living. Right thoughts produce right actions. God's ways and thoughts, which were so much higher than ours (before the cross), but which were given to us (on the cross), produce God's life in us.

Romans 5:18-19 in the Message Bible reads like this, *"Here it is in a nutshell: Just as one person did it wrong and got us into all this trouble with sin and death, another person did it right and got us out of it. But more than just getting us out of trouble, he got us into life! One man said no to God and put many people in the wrong; one man said yes to God and put many in the right."*

A couple of things here: First, the trouble we were in before the cross was with sin and death. Not with an angry God. Second, Jesus got us out of trouble and into HIS Life! Adam said no to God--and to God's way and thoughts--and this produced sin and death. Jesus said yes to God's way and thoughts. Jesus got rid of the Old Heaven and the Old Earth and the sea. He gave us a New Heaven and a New Earth!

It starts at the top and flows down. I'll end this chapter with Psalm 133.

"A Song of degrees of David. Behold, how good and how pleasant it is for the brethren to dwell together in unity. It is like the precious ointment upon the head, that ran down upon the beard, even Aaron's beard: that went down to the skirts of his garments; As the dew of Hermon, and as the dew that descended upon the mountains of Zion: for there the LORD commanded the blessing, even life for evermore."

Chapter 8

The Mountain

The precious ointment, the oil of anointing, flowed down from the mountains of Zion. NOT from Mount Sinai. This is one of the issues I think we have when it comes to realizing our EPIC destiny: We are focused on the wrong mountain.

Mount Sinai is where the Law was given. Mount Zion is the city of David. And as we know, the Seed of David is Christ. This the difference between the two mountains according to John 1:17, *"For the law was given by Moses, but grace and truth came by Jesus Christ."*

The Law vs Grace. Bondage vs. Freedom. Moses vs. Jesus. And, look, I realize Moses was doing his part. I'm not saying Jesus is AGAINST Moses. I'm not saying the Law is sin. The Law is holy. But, bottom line, it is from the wrong mountain. There's no anointing flowing from the Law. In fact, look at what Scripture says about the glory of the Law.

2 Corinthians 3:4-17, *"And such trust have we through Christ to God-ward: Not that we are sufficient of ourselves to think any thing as of ourselves; but our sufficiency is of God; Who also hath made us able ministers of the new testament; not of the letter, but of the spirit: for the letter killeth, but the spirit giveth life. But if the ministration of death, written and engraven in stones, was glorious, so that the children of Israel could not steadfastly behold the face of Moses for the glory of his countenance; which glory was to be done away: How shall not the*

ministration of the spirit be rather glorious? For if the ministration of condemnation be glory, much more doth the ministration of righteousness exceed in glory. For even that which was made glorious had no glory in this respect, by reason of the glory that excelleth. For it that which is done away was glorious, much more that which remaineth is glorious. Seeing then that we have such hope, we use great plainness of speech: And not as Moses, which put a vail over his face, that the children of Israel could not stedfastly look to the end of that which is abolished: But their minds were blinded: for until this day remaineth the same vail untaken away in the reading of the old testament; which vail is done away in Christ. But even unto his day, when Moses is read, the vail is upon their heart. Nevertheless when it shall turn to the Lord, the vail shall be taken away. Now the Lord is that Spirit: and where the Spirit of the Lord is, there is liberty."

Shew! There's a lot there. Ok. When Moses went up Mount Sinai and fasted forty days and forty nights (this fact will be important in a minute), God gave him the Law. God gave Moses the Ten Commandments. And when Moses came down the mountain his face shone. Exodus 34:29, *"And it came to pass, when Moses came down from mount Sinai with the two tables of testimony in Moses' hand, when he came down from the mount, that Moses wist not that the skin of his face shone while he talked with him."* This caused the people to run from Moses. So he put a vail on his face so they wouldn't be afraid.

But there was another reason he put a vail on his face. He didn't want the people to see that glory that came with the Law was fading. See, there's limited success that can come with trying to keep the Law. You can modify your behavior a little bit for a little while. But it's not real. It's not permanent. Because the bottom line with the Law is that it demands perfection without being able to produce perfection. It doesn't show you what you do right, it shows you what you do wrong.

The Law, the Old Covenant, Mount Sinai, is the ministry of condemnation. It's all about what you're doing, and more specifically, what you're doing wrong. That's the problem. No matter how hard you try, you can't live up to the impossible standard set by the Law. And here's another problem, Moses GAVE the Law. He put that yoke on the people. This is what religion does. It sets up hoops and demands that we jump through them in order to please God. And when we can't measure up to this standard, the result is frustration and condemnation. The result is that, just like the people of Israel, we run FROM God instead of running TO Him!

This vail that Moses wore, and really the fact that he went up to the mountain by himself, is a picture of separation. God wanted all of the people to meet with him, but they told Moses to go up the mountain, get a message from God, and bring it back to them. This isn't what God wanted, though. The cry of God's heart is, and has always been, for us to be His people and for Him to be our God.

Mount Sinai is all about us wanting to get to God on our own merits. We want to ascend to heaven. And, seemingly, Moses gave us a way to do that. "Keep the Law and you can get where you want to go." It's the same lie the serpent told Eve, "Eat from the tree of knowledge of good and evil and you can be like God." It's a work based, man-centered mountain. It's an Old Covenant.

And it's obsolete.

We started our passage with 2 Corinthians 3:4-5, *"And such trust have we through Christ to God-ward. Not that we are sufficient of ourselves to think any thing as of ourselves; but our sufficiency is of God."* Before the cross it was all about human effort. Adam stepped out of a Finished Work, and into a dimension of performance. But, again, that was before the cross.

Our EPIC destiny is not to earn our bread by the sweat of our brows. The bread of heaven is Jesus, and we don't have to earn it at all! Jesus did the work. Jesus kept the Law, every jot and every tittle. And He did it both for us and as us.

See, because there's another mountain. We are no longer standing at the foot of Mount Sinai, waiting for a list of rules to follow. No. We are enjoying the anointing that flows from Mount Zion!

Psalm 2:6 says, *"Yet have I set my king upon my holy hill of Zion."* This sums up where we live now, on this side of the cross. The holy hill of Zion, where God has set His king... King Jesus!

My book, "Six Steps to the Throne," shows us that we are in the Throne, because the Throne is in us. We don't need to ascend to Mount Zion, God set us there. When Jesus sat down at the right hand of the Father, we were in Him (because He is in us). That means that we are, right now, presently, seated in heavenly places in Christ Jesus.

Look at Galatians 4:21-31, *"Tell me, ye that desire to be under the law, do ye not hear the law? For it is written, that Abraham had two sons, the one by a bondmaid, the other by a freewoman. But he who was of the bondwoman was born after the flesh; but he of the freewoman was by promise. Which things are an allegory: for these are the two covenants; the one from the mount Sinai, which gendereth to bondage, which is Agar. For this Agar is mount Sinai in Arabia, and answereth to Jerusalem which now is, and is in bondage with her children. But Jerusalem which is above is free, which is the mother of us all. For it is written, Rejoice, thou barren that bearest not; break forth and cry, thou that travailest not: for the desolate hath many more children than she which hath an husband. Now we, brethren, as Isaac was, are the children of promise. But as then he that was born after the flesh persecuted him that was born after the Spirit, even so it is now. Nevertheless what saith the scripture? Cast out the bondwoman and her son: for the son of the bondwoman shall not be heir with the son of the freewoman. So then, brethren, we are not children of the bondwoman, but of the free."*

Remember I kept promising to get into Isaac and Ishmael? Here we go. Abraham had two sons, but God only acknowledged one of them. God did not acknowledge the son of the bondwoman. In fact, He cast out the bondwoman and her son. Because even though there are two mountains (or two Covenants, or two seeds) God is only interested in Jesus. Isaac, a type and shadow of Jesus, was the child of promise. The seed of faith.

Isaac represents Mount Zion, the holy hill where God has set His King. Isaac represents freedom. Freedom from the Law. Freedom from bondage. Freedom from the Old Covenant. Freedom from sin and death. Freedom from everything and anything that would hold you back from God's gift of eternal life.

And here, again, is the key: Ishmael was born into bondage. We didn't sin, our natural father Adam did. And because of his original sin, we were all born into sin. A seed can only produce after its own kind. Because of Adam we were born into bondage. We were born into a dimension of sin and death. Romans 5:12, *"Wherefore, as by one man sin entered into the world, and death by sin; and so death passed upon all men, for that all have sinned."*

But Isaac wasn't born into bondage. He was born of the freewoman. He wasn't born on Mount Sinai, he was born on Mount Zion!

We've already seen that this is what happens in the waters of baptism. We die to the first death by dying the second death. And we are reborn. Born not from below, but born from above. No longer is Adam our father, but God is our true heavenly Father! We are remembered, or regenerated, or put back together with a new set of genes! We are given the DNA (Divine Nature of the Almighty)! And we are born free!

There are only three ways you can legally join a family: You can be born into a family, you can marry into a family, or you can be adopted. In the Scripture all three of these dimensions of our relationship with God are covered.

John 3:3-6, *"Jesus answered and said unto him, Verily, verily, I say unto thee, Except a man be born again, he cannot see the kingdom of God. Nicodemus saith unto him, How can a man be born when he is old? can he enter the second time into his mother's womb, and be born? Jesus answered, Verily, verily, I say unto thee, Except a man be born of the water and of the Spirit, he cannot enter into the kingdom of God. That which is born of the flesh is flesh; and that which is born of the Spirit is spirit."*

Our whole EPIC destiny is tied up in our understanding of this new birth. This new, incorruptible seed. We can't enter the Kingdom unless we're born again. That's one way to "get into the family."

Revelation 21:9-10, *"And there came unto me one of the seven angels which had the seven vials full of the last seven plagues, and talked with me, saying, Come hither, I will shew thee the bride, the Lamb's wife. And he carried me away in the spirit to a great and high mountain, and shewed me that great city, the holy Jerusalem, descending out of heaven from God."*

The Lamb's wife, New Jerusalem, descended out of heaven from God. This is what happened on the cross. Babylon, a type and shadow of the world, was traded in for New Jerusalem. Mount Sinai lost its power and importance and was overshadowed by Mount Zion. Death was swallowed up by life. And, according to Revelation 11:15, *"...the kingdoms of this world are become the kingdoms of our Lord, and of his Christ; and he shall reign for ever and ever."*

We are this mountain. We are this city. On the cross we were the bride of Christ, and now we are the Lamb's wife! The city isn't a physical city. It's a people. It's us! We are the church. We are the temple. Jesus said the Kingdom of God is within you (Luke 17:21). This means that when we entered into the Kingdom, the Kingdom entered into us! Or, rather, what was planted in us has started to come out. The incorruptible seed has begun to bring forth fruit. And the fruit of the Spirit is love!

The final way to legally join a family is to be adopted into it. Romans 8:14-15 tells us, *"For as many as are led by the Spirit of God, they are the sons of God. For ye have not received the spirit of bondage again to fear; but ye have received the Spirit of adoption, whereby we cry, Abba, Father."*

Now let's work on this one for a minute. Because I don't believe our adoption into God's family is the same as we think of human adoption in the natural. I don't believe there was a time that we were ever NOT a part of God's family. Luke 3:38 identifies Adam as the son of God. But, again, there are two sons. Two mountains. Two covenants. So while we were always a son of God with a little "s," we had to be "adopted" by the Spirit in order to be the Son of God with a capital "S!"

The word, "adoption" is G5206 is Strong's Concordance and it means, "the placing as a son." It has connotations to entering into the family business. And this is one of the differences between Adam and Jesus. Adam wanted to do things his way. Jesus, even as a young boy, knew that He was placed as a Son. Luke 2:49, *"And he said unto them, How is it that ye sought me? wist ye not that I must be about my Father's business?"*

So while even though Ishmael was Abraham's son--just like Adam, and just like us before the cross--there had to be a rebirth, or a marriage, or an adoption. Something had to happen in order for us to be able to switch mountains.

What happened was the cross.

On the cross, Mount Sinai passed away and Mount Zion came forth. The Old Covenant passed away and the New Covenant came forth. Everything changed. Everything shifted. The focus stopped being on Adam (and us, his offspring) and what Adam could accomplish, and it started to be on Jesus, and what He did both for us and as us. The focus shifted from the old, corruptible seed, to the new, incorruptible seed.

Jesus said, *"Think not that I am come to destroy the law, or the prophets: I am not come to destroy, but to fulfill"* (Matthew 5:17). This is important. Because, again, God's Law is holy. I know sometimes it seems that I'm anti-Law, but I'm not. What I am is anti-trying to KEEP the Law. Because it's impossible to keep, and it was never meant for us to keep in the first place. Jesus came and fulfilled the Law. And once He did that He took it out of the way.

The Law, or the Old Covenant, or Mount Sinai, had become a stumbling block for God's people. It had become a weight that dragged people down. It had become a ministry of condemnation, and instead of keeping us from sinning, it was only able to show us what miserable sinners we were.

So Jesus fulfilled it. And according to Colossians 2:14 He also blotted out the handwriting of ordinances that was against us, which was contrary to us, and took it out of the way, nailing it to his cross. The Law was against us, and contrary to us. It demanded perfection, but couldn't produce perfection. All it could produce was guilt and condemnation, and shame, and frustration. All the Law did was give us a picture of a God who got mad at us and punished us when we messed up.

Jesus took it out of the way. He fulfilled it. Once something is fulfilled, you don't keep trying to fulfill it. If I owe the bank a hundred dollars, and then pay them one hundred dollars, I've fulfilled the obligation of that debt. I don't keep paying them though. I set the fulfilled debt aside and continue on with my life. This is exactly what Hebrews 12:1-2 instructs us to do.

"Wherefore seeing we also are compassed about with so great a cloud of witnesses, let us lay aside every weight, and the sin which doth so easily beset us, and let us run with patience the race that is set before us, Looking unto Jesus the author and finisher of our faith; who for the joy that was set before him endured the cross, despising the shame, and is set down at the right hand of the throne of God."

The weight of thinking we are sinners holds us down. But if we can begin to see--and I'm convinced that being with other believers, or a great cloud of witnesses, can really help us to see--that Jesus paid the price we couldn't pay, then we can stop trying to pay it. When we begin to see A) that the work is finished and B) how it got finished, then we can stop trying to finish it ourselves. We can lay it aside.

Let's keep our mountain analogy going. There are two mountains, Mount Sinai and Mount Zion. Jesus told us how to deal with the mountain in the book of Matthew. He cursed the fig tree, which represents the tree of death, or human effort--I go into this in depth in Six Steps to the Throne--and He told the disciples what believing would allow them to do. *"Jesus answered and said unto them, Verily I say unto you, If ye have faith, and doubt not, ye shall not only do this which is done to the fig tree, but also if ye shall say unto this mountain, Be thou removed, and be thou cast into the sea; it shall be done"* (Matthew 21:21).

Now we preach this as if Jesus was saying, "Whatever your mountain is, if you believe hard enough, you can cast it into the sea!" We use the mountain to represent obstacles. But the mountain Jesus was talking about was Mount Sinai! He said, "ye shall say unto THIS mountain." If we can stop looking at obstacles altogether, if we stop looking at human effort all together, then we can see that the mountain that was cast into the sea is the Law! Man-centered, performance-based religion has kept us in bondage for too long.

Jesus got rid of everything that would keep us from life. He got rid of the fig tree, He got rid of sin and death, and He got rid of Mount Sinai!

Acts 22:28 tells us why it is so important that we realize that there is only one mountain left. *"And the chief captain answered, With a great sum obtained I this freedom. And Paul said, But I was free born."* See, Mount Sinai--or the Law--represents bondage. You think you can earn freedom, or liberty, or eternal life. You think through your effort, or with a great sum, you can achieve your EPIC destiny.

But you can't.

Jesus said it like this, *"And Jesus looking upon them saith, With men it is impossible, but not with God: for with God all things are possible"* (Mark 10:27). A bondservant cannot become a Son, unless he is born again. Paul didn't earn his freedom. He didn't do it himself. He was born free. Paul spent a lot of time thinking he was on Mount Sinai. And it wasn't until he met Jesus--until Jesus literally knocked him off his donkey--that Saul realized Mount Sinai had been cast into the sea. Saul was born again--born free--and became Paul! He got a new name, or a new nature! He was transformed from a servant to a Son!

There were two mountains; Mount Sinai and Mount Zion. There were two men; Adam and Jesus. But when Jesus finished the work on the Cross, when Jesus fulfilled our EPIC destiny 2,000 years ago, He cast Mount Sinai into the sea. He buried Adam. He remade the world in His image and brought us out of bondage and into His glorious liberty and freedom!

The oil of anointing doesn't flow down from Mount Sinai. It is the anointing of the King, and it flows from Mount Zion. It flows... like healing rain.

Chapter 9

Healing Rain

I don't want to mix my metaphors here, or paint a confusing picture, but the truth of the matter is that healing rain is almost a misnomer. Because an understanding of the finished work reveals to us the truth that we don't need healing at all. We ARE healed. But sometimes it doesn't feel like we're healed. Sometimes it feels like we need healing to flow, or fall, like rain. So we're going to look at the rain, and see what it means that the rain has already fallen.

The thing I hope we've been seeing is that it's all about Jesus, and it's all about love. Everything we're talking about is a consuming fire that feeds on itself. Love feeds on love. So before we talk about the rain, let's talk about fire.

Exodus 3:2-4, *"And the angel of the LORD appeared unto him in a flame of fire out of the midst of a bush: and he looked, and, behold, the bush burned with fire, and the bush was not consumed. And Moses said, I will now turn aside, and see this great sight, why the bush is not burnt. And when the LORD saw that he turned aside to see, God called unto him out of the midst of the bush, and said, Moses, Moses. And he said, Here am I."*

Notice the important thing about the bush--it was burning, but it wasn't consumed. Moses was on the backside of the desert. It wasn't extraordinary for a bush to be on fire. What was different about this bush, though, was that it was burning, but it wasn't being burnt. It was on fire, but it wasn't being destroyed.

Now look at what Jesus says in Matthew 7:19, *"Every tree that bringeth not forth good fruit is hewn down, and cast into the fire."* Unfortunately, tragically, we preach this verse as, "If you're a sinner God is going to throw you into hell for eternity." God--who IS a consuming fire--doesn't burn to destroy people. He burns (with love) to purify people! In this case I believe we can see the trees that bringeth not forth good fruit not as PEOPLE, but as thoughts, or mindsets, or wrong believing. Guys... what you believe dictates what you do. It's not actions God is concerned about, but WHY you do the things you do. God is concerned with your heart. That's why He gave you HIS heart!

Right believing produces right living. Wrong believing needs to be cast into the fire (which is God) so that the wrong believing can be consumed, but the believer won't be burnt!

We're talking about fire to show that love feeds on love without consuming love. To show that in order for love to grow, anything that isn't love needs to be purified. And, again, we're not talking about getting rid of people who misbehave. We're talking about getting rid of anything IN people that isn't love!

And really we're talking about a finished work, so we're talking about revealing to people that this purifying already happened. The consuming fire already burned away everything that wasn't love. Jesus already remade the world in His image. The fire already burned. And the rain already fell.

The Bible talks about rain a lot. And it talks about clouds a lot. Here's the first thing to realize: WE are the clouds. WE carry the rain.

2 Peter chapter 2 talks at length about "natural brute beasts," who, "...are wells without water, clouds that are carried with a tempest; to whom the mist of darkness is reserved for ever" (2 Peter 2:17). But I don't want to spend time on this... because it doesn't apply to you. And it

doesn't apply to me. The natural brute beasts are those in darkness. And we are the light of the world!

So let's instead turn our attention to the rain that we ARE filled with. The water that DOES flow through us.

Here's a key: The first time it rained on the earth was the flood. And here's what God said about the flood, *"And, behold, I, even I, do bring a flood of waters upon the earth, to destroy all flesh, wherein is the breath of life, from under heaven; and everything that is in the earth shall die."* Sounds terrible, doesn't it? Sounds like an angry God punishing His creation, right? Sounds like God throwing a fit and hitting the reset button, doesn't it?

Does it? Really look at what God said. He said He was going to destroy all flesh. Flesh speaks of human effort. And God said in that human effort was the breath of life. He destroyed it because He didn't want us to have life... He wanted us to have ABUNDANT life! He didn't want us to have Adam's life of service, and bondage, living in a cursed dimension of the world. He wanted us to have Jesus' life! For God to destroy the human effort that could never earn what it desired... that's not a bad thing. That's a good thing.

God said He was going destroy everything under heaven. Again, this sounds like God is doing something bad, right? How can a good God do something bad? A house divided against itself cannot stand. God is light, and there is no darkness in Him at all. See, God destroyed everything under heaven because He didn't want us to live UNDER heaven. He wanted us to live IN heaven!

And remember the first covenant? God put Noah in the Ark, so that when the flood came and washed the earth clean, Noah wouldn't be destroyed, he would be saved! Just like the fire that purifies, but doesn't burn the bush up, the water washed Noah, but didn't drown him! We have been washed clean by the healing rain. We were in the Ark, so when everything under heaven was destroyed, we weren't UNDER heaven, we were IN heaven!

The incorruptible seed of the Holy Spirit--or God's heart--that was planted in us on the cross, needed to be saturated with the healing rain in order to grow, and bring forth the harvest. Love was planted, and watered with love, in order to bring forth a harvest of love!

This was God's promise, as seen in Leviticus 26:3-4, *"If ye walk in my statues, and keep my commandments, and do them; Then I will give you rain in due season, and the land shall yield her increase, and the trees of the field shall yield their fruit."* Now before we start saying, "See! We have to keep the Law if we want God to bless us!" let's remember who the Bible is talking about. It's talking about Jesus.

Jesus walked in God's statues. Jesus kept God's commandments, and did them. Jesus fulfilled the Law. And that means, the due season in which God gave us the healing rain... was the cross! We don't need to earn God's rain. Jesus already did it both for us and as us!

And now that Jesus did the work--fulfilling the Law, and casting Mount Sinai into the sea, cursing the fig tree of human effort, destroying the devil and his works, killing the body of sin and death--the only tree left that can bear fruit is the Tree of Life! Every other tree was cast into the fire!

Jesus is the flood, and the Ark, and the rain. He is all in all.

Genesis chapter 7 verse 12, speaking of the flood tells us, *"And the rain was upon the earth forty days and forty nights."* This corresponds directly with Jesus' period of tempting in the wilderness after He was baptized and received the Holy Spirit. Once again, we think it's all about us, when really it's all about Jesus. The forty days and forty nights of rain were for our cleansing, but this cleansing was accomplished in Jesus! He was tempted, because He could resist the temptation! We were put in the Ark, not so we could escape the flood, but so it could do it's perfect work without destroying us!

God promised to destroy all flesh under heaven. But He put us IN heaven, and He put heaven in US! What was destroyed was not wicked people, but the WICKEDNESS of people! And what happens when it rains? The seed that was planted begins to bear fruit!

Look at Deuteronomy 32:1-4, *"Give ear, O ye heavens, and I will speak; and hear, O earth, the words of my mouth. My doctrine shall drop as rain, my speech shall distil as the dew, as the small rain upon the tender herb, and as the showers upon the grass: Because I will publish the name of the LORD: ascribe ye greatness unto our God. He is the Rock, his work is perfect: for all his ways are judgment: a God of truth and without iniquity, just and right is he."*

Moses said his doctrine shall drop as rain. The word, "doctrine," is number 3948 in Strong's Hebrew Concordance and it means, "something received, that is, instruction." So we see the two-part economy of God where He instructs us--the way of grace--and where we receive it--the walk of faith. This is vital. A gift can be given (as it was on the cross), but until it is received it doesn't do anything for anybody.

And Moses said there are many forms of this rain of doctrine. Dew, which comes in the night season and does it's work even when we aren't aware of it. The dew that was spoken of in Psalm 133:3, *"As the dew of Hermon, and as the dew that descended upon the mountains of Zion: for there the LORD commanded the blessing, even life for evermore."* See, Jesus came as a thief in the night and gave us this gift. We simply need to see the gift, receive the gift, and be the gift! Jesus came to give us the dew of life. He came to give us everlasting life. He came to manifest our EPIC destiny!

Another form of this rain is "small rain upon the tender herb." This speaks to me about not just the doctrine we preach, but the WAY we preach it. We can't force Jesus down people's throats, or they'll choke on Him. We have to be small. The Apostle Paul's name means, "little." Sometimes we don't need to quote scripture, we just need to love. Especially to unbelievers. Jesus doesn't make sense to the unregenerated mind... but love is what everybody--EVERYBODY--craves and desires and needs.

Finally, this rain of doctrine comes as showers upon the grass. It soaks and nourishes the fields. It creates the green pastures that the Shepherd makes us to lie down on. The rain is what makes things grow. The rain is what makes the seed that was planted in corruption come forth into incorruption.

There are two types of rain mentioned in Scripture: The former and the latter rain. The former rain is what softens the ground so that seed can be planted. And that latter rain is what comes in order to bring forth the harvest. Now look at Hosea 6:1-3, *"Come, and let us return unto the LORD: for he hath torn, and he will heal us; he hath smitten, and he will bind us up. After two days will he revive us: in the third day he will raise us up, and we shall live in his sight. Then shall we know, if we follow on to know the LORD: his going forth is prepared as the morning; and he shall come unto us as the rain, as the latter and former rain unto the earth."*

Right off the bat let's make sure we understand that the Bible does not say God has torn US. It says He has torn. Who did He tear? Jesus. The Bible is about Jesus, remember? God tore Jesus, and healed us. God has smitten Jesus, and He bound us up. This passage is about the cross. On the third day God raised up His Son. And since we were in Him when He died, now He is in us and we live!

Interesting too that Hosea prophesies that Jesus will come to us as the latter and former rain. It looks like he got it backwards, right? Well, that's keeping with the upside down, backwards economy of God. The way God works is, He sent the latter rain first. He brought forth the harvest on the cross. And then He sent the former rain, so that we could begin to see what the harvest is!

We were conformed to the image of Jesus on the cross. We don't need to be conformed to His image, we need to understand what His image is. The seed was not only planted on the cross, but it came to fruition. Our EPIC destiny manifested on the cross. The latter rain came, and the seed that was planted bore fruit!

This life is not about becoming anything. It is not about being conformed to anything. It is simply about finding out what we have been comformed to. It's not BECOMING anything, but finding out what we became on the cross! It's not about God changing us into the image of Jesus. He already did that. It's about finding out what the image of Jesus is. Because when we figure that out... when we see Him as He truly is, we will BE Him as He truly is!

Let's link two verses, Habakkuk 2:14, and 2 Corinthians 4:6. *"For the earth shall be filled with the knowledge of the glory of the LORD, as the waters cover the sea"* (Habakkuk 2:14). *"For God, who commanded the light to shine out of darkness, hath shined in our hearts, to give the light of the knowledge of the glory of God in the face of Jesus Christ."*

The waters cover the sea. Interesting phrase. The water, or the Word, or the doctrine, covers the sea, or the wickedness of man. And what happens when the Word covers the wickedness of man? The KNOWLEDGE of the glory of the Lord. The glory was planted on the cross. What we need is for the light to shine in our hearts so we can see who we be! Jesus is the glory of God. Jesus was planted in us on the cross. And the water of the healing rain brings forth what was planted.

Now how does this rain that already came... come? It comes when we publish the name of the Lord! When we ascribe greatness unto our God! When we preach Jesus, Jesus is what manifests. Whatever you magnify will manifest. If your focus isn't on Jesus, then you'll feel dry. Because He IS the healing rain.

Now don't misunderstand me: Whether your focus is on Jesus or it isn't, He's still there. It comes back to the gift again. Just because it has been given doesn't mean it has been received. We can either enjoy the gift, or we can reject it. It's our choice. If we want to make what's true, true for us, then we have to receive the gift. We have to receive the rain.

Go dance in the rain, and see if you can stay dry!

But here's another key: The rain has already come. The work is already finished. Christ is our Rock, and out of Him flows the living water. But God had a very specific plan regarding how the water came out of that rock.

See, the people of Israel were in the desert and they were dry. They were thirsty. They needed water. So God told Moses, *"Behold, I will stand before thee there upon the rock in Horeb; and thou shalt smite the rock, and there shall come water out of it, that the people may drink. And Moses did so in the sight of the elders of Israel"* (Exodus 17:6). God told Moses to smite the rock. This speaks of God smiting Jesus on the cross. This speaks of the work being finished.

Then, later on, the people needed water again. Numbers 20:8-12, *"Take the rod, and gather thou the assembly together, thou, and Aaron thy brother, and speak ye unto the rock before their eyes; and it shall give forth his water, and thou shalt bring forth to them water out of the rock: so thou shalt give the congregation and their beasts drink. And Moses took the rod from before the LORD, as he commanded him. And Moses and Aaron gathered the congregation together before the rock, and he said unto them, Hear now, ye rebels; must we fetch you water out of this rock? And Moses lifted up his hand, and with his rod he smote the rock twice: and the water came out abundantly, and the congregation drank, and their beasts also. And the LORD spake unto Moses and Aaron, Because ye believed me not, to sanctify me in the eyes of the children of Israel, therefore ye shall not bring this congregation into the land which I have given them."*

After the Rock was smitten, and the work was finished, God told His leader, Moses, to speak to the Rock. But Moses disobeyed God. He smote the Rock again. He didn't believe the work was finished, so he tried to finish it himself. This is the problem we find ourselves in so often. We try to bring the rain through our human efforts, without really understanding that we don't need to bring the rain at all. The rain has already come! All we need to do is speak about it. Tell people about Jesus.

And I'm convinced that what we are supposed to tell people about Jesus is NOT that He will save them if they perform right. I'm convinced that what we are supposed to tell people about Jesus is that He already saved them on the cross! Don't tell people how to get the water... tell them how the water got them!

"In the last day, that great day of the feast, Jesus stood and cried, saying, If any man thirst, let him come unto me, and drink. He that believeth on me, as the scripture hath said, out of his belly shall flow rivers of living water" (John 7:37-38). Jesus didn't say, "Come and drink or else." He said, "If you're thirsty, come and drink. And when you drink, the same living water will begin to flow out of you!"

God already sent the rain. All we have to do is drink it. All we ever have to do is receive God's love, and then we'll be able to release it. And now, on this side of the cross, because of the Holy Spirit, we are equipped and empowered to receive it and release it!

So we don't need the healing rain to come. It has already come. It flows down like the anointing oil, or dew, from Mount Zion. God sent the latter and the former rain. All of the planting, and the watering, and the harvesting, was accomplished on the cross. Our part is not smiting the Rock, it is speaking of the Rock. Our part is not producing the rain, it is drinking the water!

Chapter 10

The Rainbow

I hope we're seeing a pattern here. The seed is sown, on the right mountain, God sends the latter and the former rain, and the harvest comes forth. But what follows a really big rain? What followed the first rain--the flood?

A rainbow.

Genesis 9:12-17 in the Message Bible, *"God continued, "This is the sign of the covenant I am making between me and you and everything living around you and everyone living after you. I'm putting my rainbow in the clouds, a sign of the covenant between me and the Earth. From now on, when I form a cloud over the Earth and the rainbow appears in the cloud, I'll remember my covenant between me and you and everything living, that never again will floodwaters destroy all life. When the rainbow appears in the cloud, I'll see it and remember the eternal covenant between God and everything living, every last living creature on Earth." And God said, "This is the sign of the covenant that I've set up between me and everything living on the Earth.""*

The rainbow is God's sign of the covenant. We think of the flood as something terrible, but really it was something beautiful, and it is marked by something beautiful. God washed the world clean. And then He promised never to do it again. He smote the Rock once. He finished the work. And He sealed it with a rainbow.

This is awesome to me. Look where the rainbow is: "I'm putting my rainbow in the clouds." Who are the clouds? WE ARE!!! God sealed His covenant IN US!

When this rainbow--this light that shines after the rain--is formed in the clouds, then God remembers His covenant. When Jesus manifests in us, God knows--and more importantly WE know--that God put us in the Ark when He put the Ark in us! Our EPIC destiny comes to life when the rainbow shines in the clouds.

Ezekiel 1:28 picks this thought up, *"As the appearance of the bow that is in the cloud in the day of rain, so was the appearance of the brightness round about. This was the appearance of the likeness of the glory of the LORD..."*

The rainbow is God's glory shining in and through His people! And, amazingly enough, this glory of God, this rainbow, is the very image of Jesus! This is the image that we have been conformed into! Colossians 1:15 declares that Jesus, *"...is the image of the invisible God..."*

Jesus showed us what God looks like. And what He showed us-- we're really going to get into this later on--is love in a body. That is the image of Jesus Christ. That is the image that was our EPIC destiny to be conformed into. That is what God looks like... and that is what we look like!

On the mountain of transfiguration Jesus took three disciples with Him to see the glory of God. Matthew 17:1-2, *"And after six days Jesus taketh Peter, James, and John his brother, and bringeth them up into an high mountain apart, And was transfigured before them: and his face did shine as the sun, and his raiment was white as the light."*

The rainbow literally shined in the cloud that day. God remembered His covenant. And watch this: The three disciples Jesus brought, and revealed the image and glory of God to, also clarified what covenant, and what mountain we are dealing with! Peter means, "Stone." James means, "Replace." And John means, "Grace."

The stone of the Law was replaced by grace!

God was using His Son's transfiguration, the shining of the rainbow, to bring us back to the original covenant. Jesus made the old things pass away and He made all things new. The flood washed away the wickedness of man, and brought forth the righteousness of God in Christ Jesus!

In fact, if we continue the story of the mount of transfiguration--the word, "transfigured" means, "transformed," by the way--we see that Peter (the Stone) wanted to build three tabernacles and include Moses and Elijah, the Law and the Prophets, in the equation. But God interrupted Peter and said, *"...This is my beloved Son, in whom I am well pleased; hear ye him"* (Matthew 17:5).

God said, "No, no, no. It's not Jesus and the Law and the Prophets. It's not the Old and the New Covenant. It's not Mount Sinai and Mount Zion. It's Jesus all by Himself."

We don't need the Law anymore, once we understand who we are, because it is the schoolmaster that brings us to Christ. Once it does its job, it's no longer necessary. God made the Old Covenant with the people of Israel because THEY wanted a set of rules to follow. God met them where they were at. But God's ORIGINAL covenant was, "I'm going to put you in the Ark and destroy all flesh though a flood of healing rain."

This is the covenant that was sealed with the shining of God's glory. And when we understand this original covenant, we will understand that the New Covenant was really a return to God's original plan. The New Covenant isn't God's plan B. God doesn't have a plan B., because He doesn't need a plan B.

He gave the people an Old Covenant to show them that they couldn't do it on their own. They wanted to try it themselves, so God let them. But He knew that covenant wasn't going to last. How could it, when it couldn't accomplish what it was meant to do?

God had to let us see that we needed a savior. He had to let us get to the end of our rope, so to speak, so that we could see that OUR rope doesn't go anywhere. Once again, with man it is impossible, but with God all things are possible.

Man by himself cannot conform to Jesus' image. Man by himself cannot fulfill his EPIC destiny. Man by himself is a corruptible seed.

God's rainbow doesn't remind God of His covenant with us, as much as it reminds US of God's covenant with us. Jesus had to get the Law out of the way in order to free us from that bondage. Jesus took us out from under the Law, and brought us into grace. And look at what that means:

"For sin shall not have dominion over you: for ye are not under the law, but under grace" (Romans 6:14).

The only thing the Law produces is more lawbreakers. The only thing the Old Covenant did was condemn people, and bring their sins to remembrance. Jesus, who is God's grace, took away the sin of the world. He transformed us from sinners to saints! He brought us out of the world, through the flood, and into the Kingdom!

And what would a Kingdom be without a Throne? For about 200 pages about the Throne, check out my book, "Six Steps to the Throne." For our purposes regarding the rainbow and the throne, check out Revelation 4:2-3, *"And immediately I was in the spirit: and, behold, a throne was set in heaven, and one sat on the throne. And he that sat was to look upon like a jasper and a sardine stone: and there was a rainbow round about the throne, in sight like unto an emerald."*

The throne is in heaven. The rainbow surrounds the throne. We are in heaven, because heaven is in us. That means the we are in the throne, because the throne is in us. That means the throne--where the King sits--

is in us. It is the heart of God, the incorruptible seed, beating in our chest. And what surrounds God's heart in our chest? His glory!

What am I trying to say? 2 Peter 1:19 sums it up for me. *"We have also a more sure word of prophecy; whereunto ye do well that ye take heed, as unto a light that shineth in a dark place, until the day dawn, and the day star arise in your hearts."*

We have a more sure word of prophecy. We know exactly what God is up to, because we know exactly what God accomplished on the cross! We know that our EPIC destiny is not in jeopardy, because it has already come to pass!

What we need is not the glory of God, but the KNOWELDGE of the glory of God. What we need is not a move of God, but a revelation of Jesus. We don't need God to move, we need to know what happened when He moved 2,000 years ago! This is what the rainbow represents. It is our reminder that God's glory--His grace, and His mercy, and His truth, and His love--lives in us!

The rainbow is around the throne. The rainbow heralds the King, who is seated in His throne, ruling and reigning in and through us. The rainbow comes after the rain and shines forth the glory of God. What an awesome picture.

Revelation 21:10-11 makes this connection yet again. *"And he carried me away in the spirit to a great and high mountain, and shewed me that great city, the holy Jerusalem, descending out of heaven from God, Having the glory of God: and her light was like unto a stone most precious, even like a jasper stone, clear as crystal."* In Revelation chapter 4, He that sat on the throne was like jasper. In Revelation 21 it is the Lamb's Wife, the holy Jerusalem, that is likened to a jasper stone. And the jasper stone is shining with the glory of God!

Revelation chapter 10 mentions the rainbow again. Revelation 10:1-3, *"And I saw another mighty angel come down from heaven, clothed with a cloud: and a rainbow was upon his head, and his face was as it were the sun, and his feet as pillars of fire: And he had in his hand a little book open: and he set his right foot upon the sea, and his left foot on the earth. And cried with a loud voice, as when a lion roareth: and when he had cried, seven thunders uttered their voices."*

There's the connection between the rainbow and the clouds again. He, Jesus, was clothed with clouds. He lives in us. We are His many-membered body. And the rainbow, or glory of God, was upon His head. God's glory is in our minds. It's in our belief in Jesus!

His face shines the glory that is upon His head. We are what we believe. And His feet are pillars of fire. Everywhere He walks--the earth and the sea--is consumed by His purifying love! Wickedness and human effort are swallowed up in Jesus, just as sin and death are swallowed up in His life!

The glory of God is what transformed us, and the glory of God is what we were transformed into.

Moses, the mediator of the Old Covenant, asked God for something in Exodus 33:18, *"And he said, I beseech the, shew me thy glory."* This is the same cry that king David had. They wanted God's heart, or His glory. But, because the cross hadn't yet happened, and the Holy Spirit didn't yet live in people, it was a request that God couldn't--at the time--give them. God answered Moses, *"And he said, Thou canst not see my face: for there shall no man see me, and live. And the LORD said, Behold, there is a place by me, and thou shalt stand upon a rock: And it shall come to pass, while my glory passeth by, that I will put thee in a clift of the rock, and will cover thee with my hand while I pass by: And I will take away mine hand, and thou shalt see my back parts: but my face shall not be seen"* (Exodus 33:20-23).

This is the problem with the Law: It doesn't show you the glory of God. It shows you a disappointed God who walks away from you.

But there is redemption here too. God said He would put Moses in the rock. That means Jesus. And God said He would cover Moses' face with His hand. This is the five-fold ministry. God was setting things in place, even back then.

Ephesians 4:11-13, *"And he gave some, apostles; and some, prophets; and some, evangelists; and some pastors and teachers; For the perfecting of the saints, for the work of the ministry, for the edifying of the body of Christ: Till we all come in the unity of the faith, and of the knowledge of the Son of God, unto a perfect man, unto the measure of the stature of the fulness of Christ."*

God's hand on our face is what brings us into the unity of faith. It brings us into the KNOWLEDGE of the Son of God. It brings us into the KNOWLEDGE of who we are. Jesus said, *"Howbeit when he, the Spirit of truth, is come, he will guide you into all truth..."* (John 16:13).

All truth is our EPIC destiny! All truth is that God loves us! All truth is that we have the glory of God, and that we ARE the glory of God!

Now watch this: Remember who showed up on the mount of transfiguration? Moses! Under the Old Covenant no man could see God's face and live. No man could see God's glory. So Moses had to die, and the Law had to pass off the scene. As grace replaced the Law, Moses looked God right in the face, and beheld His glory!

Moses looked Jesus right in the eye, with an open face--no vail of the Law--and He saw God's glory. And according to 2 Corinthians 3:18, when we see God as He truly is--when we look in the mirror and see that He is in us--we are changed from glory to glory! We become what we behold.

We step into our EPIC Destiny, not by trying to conform to the image of Jesus, but by seeing Him as He truly is, and in so doing we see ourselves as we truly are! When we look in the mirror and see Jesus, we can start to understand that WE ARE JESUS! We ARE conformed to His image!

108

Chapter 11

Corn, Wine, and Oil

All of these analogies about sowing and reaping, about planting and harvesting, are leading us to one thing: The fruit of the Spirit. But before we talk about fruit, we need to talk about the firstfruit, or the tithe.

But don't worry, I'm not after your money. If you bought this book, you're already supporting my ministry with your money AND your support. What I'm talking about when it comes to the tithe is... believe it or not... Jesus.

Remember our key verse for this whole book? Romans 8:29, *"For whom he did foreknow, he also did predestinate to be conformed to the image of his Son, that he might be the firstborn among many brethren."* Jesus is the firstborn. The last--Jesus--has become first, and the first--Adam--has become last. See, even though Adam was born first, he isn't the firstborn. And really, he wasn't "born" first at all. Adam was created out of the dust of the ground.

Technically, Cain was the first man born from a man and a woman. And he was of the corruptible seed. His twin brother, Abel, who came after him, was the incorruptible seed. This is the same principal we see with Ishmael and Isaac, and with Adam and Jesus. There was a natural birth first, but it isn't as important as the spiritual birth.

Colossians 1:18 in the Amplified Bible says it like this, *"He also is the Head of [His] body, the church; seeing He is the Beginning, the*

Firstborn from among the dead, so that He alone in everything and in every respect might occupy the chief place [stand first and be preeminent]."

Jesus is the firstborn of the dead. He is the firstborn from above. He is the firstborn, not to life, but to Resurrection Life. When Jesus remade the world in His image on the cross, when He died, and was buried, and rose again, He changed the whole ballgame. The corruptible seed was planted, and the incorruptible seed was harvested!

Now watch how powerful this is: Romans 11:16 says, *"For if the firstfruit be holy, the lump also is holy: and if the root be holy, so are the branches."* Jesus, the firstfruit, sowed Himself in corruption, so that He could reap US in incorruption! We are holy because He is holy! We are holy because the Holy One lives inside us! We are perfect because the Perfect One lives in us!

Romans 11:16 is one of two times the word, "firstfruit" appears in the King James version of the Bible. The other time is in Deuteronomy 18:4. Let's look at Deuteronomy 18:3-5 to get the story.

"And this shall be the priest's due from the people, from them that offer a sacrifice, whether it be ox or sheep; and they shall give unto the priest the shoulder, and the two cheeks, and the maw. The firstfruit also of thy corn, of thy wine, and of thine oil, and the first of the fleece of thy sheep, shalt thou give him. For the LORD thy God hath chosen him out of all thy tribes, to stand to minister in the name of the LORD, him and his sons forever."

Part of the Law of Moses demanded that the people give offerings to the Levitical priesthood. They had to give the firstfruit of their corn, wine, oil, and sheep. Now the word, "firstfruit," is H7225 in Strong's Concordance and it means, "the first, in place, time, order or rank. Beginning, chief, principal thing." Basically, it means the best. The best of your corn, wine, oil, and sheep belonged to the priesthood. Under that economy you had to give the best you had to religion.

You had to tithe, or you would be under a curse. You had to perform, or blessings weren't coming your way. It was all about what YOU did, rather than what JESUS did. But looking through the eyes of grace, and looking through the cross, we can see that everything required by religion, the corn, the wine, the oil, and the lamb... IS Jesus!

John 12:23-26, *"And Jesus answered them, saying, The hour is come, that the Son of man should be glorified. Verily, verily, I say unto you, Except a corn of wheat fall into the ground and die, it abideth alone: but if it die, it bringeth forth much fruit. He that loveth his life shall lose it; and he that hateth his life in this world shall keep it unto life eternal. If any man serve me, let him follow me; and where I am, there shall also my servant be: if any man serve me, him will my Father honour."*

Jesus is the corn. And He knew that only by dying--by being planted in corruption--could He bring forth much fruit. Here's the key though: He says, "If any man serve me, let him follow me; and where I am, there shall also my servant be." He was saying, "My death is your death. And if you identify with My death, then you can have My Life!"

The firstfruit of the corn that God demanded... was Jesus. And as we look at the tithe, the sacrifice, we need to understand that when Jesus fulfilled all of these demands He did it once and for all. *"For by one offering he hath perfected for ever them that are sanctified"* (Hebrews 10:14). He is the only offering God respected and accepted. He didn't just cover our sin, He took it away. He didn't just fulfill the Law, He put it aside and established a new law; the perfect law of liberty. He didn't just die FOR us, He died AS us!

When Jesus told Nicodemus that he had to be born again, this is what He was talking about. He wasn't telling Nicodemus something that Nicodemus had to do... He was telling Nicodemus what HE was going to do on the cross! The corn of wheat died, and was born again from above! The firstfruit (Jesus) is holy, and that makes the lump (us) holy! We can only be born again, or born from above, because Jesus died and rose again. We don't really DO anything, we just believe that Jesus did everything!

So Jesus is the corn. He is the first born and the firstfruit. He is also the wine.

Matthew 26:26-29, *"And as they were eating, Jesus took bread, and blessed it, and brake it, and gave it to the disciples, and said, Take, eat; this is my body. And he took the cup, and gave thanks, and gave it to them, saying, Drink ye all of it; For this is my blood of the new testament, which is shed for many for the remission of sins. But I say unto you, I will not drink henceforth of this fruit of the vine, until that day when I drink it new with you in my Father's kingdom."*

The wine is the blood of Jesus. And on the cross it was shed for us. But, again, it's about total identification. Jesus told His disciples to drink all of it. This echoes the command that was given at the first Passover to eat the whole lamb. It's not enough to be a "follower" of Jesus. It can't be us trying to walk in Jesus' footsteps. It has to be Jesus walking in our feet!

And Jesus said He wouldn't drink the wine again until He drank it with us in the Kingdom. Fast forward a little bit to the cross. John 19:29-30 (MSG), *"A jug of sour wine was standing by. Someone put a sponge soaked with the wine on a javelin and lifted it to his mouth. After he took the wine, Jesus said, "It's done... complete." Bowing his head, he offered us his spirit."*

Jesus drank wine again on the cross! The Kingdom came right then and there! The tithe was given--the ultimate, final sacrifice that the Old Covenant demanded--and Jesus said, "It is finished!" He translated us out of the power of darkness and into His Kingdom!

Here's the thing about wine though--especially new wine--it has to go into new bottles. The New Covenant isn't for the Old Man. The Kingdom is for the King.

Luke 5:37-39, *"And no man putteth new wine into old bottles; else the new wine will burst the bottles, and be spilled, and the bottles shall perish. But new wine must be put into new bottles; and both are preserved. No man also having drunk old wine straightaway desireth new: for he saith, The old is better."*

The new wine--the blood of Jesus--runs through the veins of the New Man. God's heart beats in our chest--and it beats with love--but we have to understand who we are. We have to understand that this Christian life is not about modifying the behavior of Adam. The first, Adam, has become last. It's not about the Old Man anymore, because He died. The last, Jesus, has become first. It's ALL about Jesus.

Those who drink the old wine--the Old Covenant, or religion--can't accept the new wine. It doesn't fit in their bottle. A God of mercy and grace and love doesn't fit into their idea of "an eye for an eye." Human justice demands that we get what we deserve. But on the cross Jesus got what we deserved so that we could get what HE deserved! Jesus took it all so we could get it all.

God wants the best for you... and that's why He put the best (Jesus) IN you!

Trying to mix Law and grace doesn't work. Trying to get the new wine to fit into the old bottle doesn't work. There was a shift, and a change, and a complete transformation that took place on the cross. Out with the old and in with Jesus!

Jesus is the corn, and the wine. He is the firstfruit and the tithe. He is the oil.

I hope we've shown by now that the oil is the Holy Spirit--Jesus' Spirit. So let's look at a parable Jesus told in order to show the power and the significance of the oil.

Matthew 25:1-13, *"Then shall the kingdom of heaven be likened unto ten virgins, which took their lamps, and went forth to meet the bridegroom. And five of them were wise, and five were foolish. They that were foolish took their lamps, and took no oil with them: But the wise took oil in their vessels with their lamps. While the bridegroom tarried, they all slumbered and slept. And at midnight there was a cry made, Behold, the bridegroom cometh; go ye out to meet him. Then all those virgins arose, and trimmed their lamps. And the foolish said unto the wise, Give us of your oil; for our lamps are gone out. But the wise answered, saying, Not so; lest there be not enough for us and you: but go ye rather to them that sell, and buy for yourselves. And while they went to buy, the bridegroom came; and they that were ready went in with him to the marriage: and the door was shut. Afterward came also the other virgins, saying, Lord, Lord, open to us. But he answered and said, Verily I say unto you, I know you not. Watch therefore, for ye know neither the day nor the hour wherein the Son of man cometh."*

On the surface it sounds like a pretty simple, if harsh, story. If you have oil and keep your light shining, you'll get into heaven, and if you don't... well... you won't. Right?

There are a couple things to notice though. Both the foolish and the wise virgins slumbered and slept. Having the oil or not having it didn't change the situation they all found themselves in. This life is not about circumstances. It's not what you're in... it's what's in you!

Having the oil--or the Holy Spirit--doesn't change the fact that you're still in this world, so to speak. What it does is it allows you to be IN the world, but not OF the world. That's why Jesus said, *"These things I have spoken unto you, that in me ye might have peace. In the world ye shall have tribulation: but be of good cheer; I have overcome the world"* (John 16:33). THAT'S what the oil does. It let's your light shine no matter how dark it seems.

Now when the bridegroom came the foolish virgins wanted some of the wise virgins' oil. And the wise virgins told them to go buy some. Without the Holy Spirit all you have is religion, where you have to work and earn everything you get. Paul said it was foolish to try to finish in the flesh what was started in the Spirit (Galatians 3:3), but this is so

114

often what we try to do. We don't trust the Holy Spirit, we trust our own flesh, or human effort.

So when the bridegroom comes, the foolish virgins are shut out of the marriage, and the wise virgins--those with the oil, that kept their lamps burning--are brought into the New Covenant. This is not a story of sinners vs. saints. It is a story of the Old and New Covenants. It is a story of religion vs. relationship.

The oil was given as a gift. But if you don't receive it, you'll miss out on it. And if you try to earn it, you won't be able to get the oil, or the marriage.

Jesus is the corn, the wine, and the oil. He is the firstfruit, and the tithe.

The word tithe means, "tenth." That's where we get the principal of giving ten percent of what we earn to the church. But I want to show you a couple of things regarding what WE do, and what God WANTS us to do.

Genesis 14:18-20, *"And Melchizedek king of Salem brought forth bread and wine: and he was the priest of the most high God. And he blessed him, and said, Blessed be Abram of the most high God, possessor of heaven and earth: And blessed be the most high God, which hath delivered thine enemies into thy hand. And he gave him tithes of all."*

We think if we tithe, we will get the blessing, or the victory. But here's the real order: God gave Abram the victory. God gave Abram bread and wine (the body and the blood of Jesus). God did it all. THEN Abram gave tithes of all.

Here's a key that we must understand: You can't give something you don't have. In order to give a tithe... you must first receive something from the Lord. In order to tithe the corn, wine, and oil... you first have to HAVE the corn, wine, and oil. Jesus is the firstfruit, and the tithe, and unless we receive him we cannot release Him!

Look at what Jesus says about the tithe in Luke 11:42, *"But woe unto you, Pharisees! for ye tithe mint and rue and all manner of herbs, and pass over judgment and the love of God: these ought ye to have done, and not to leave the other undone."* Jesus says judgment and the love of God--and the judgment of God IS His love--are more important than what material objects you give.

I'm not saying money isn't important; it takes money to run ministry, and Ecclesiastes 10:19 says, *"...money answereth all things."* But I hope we're seeing that while money is important, it's not the most important thing. Money is NOT the root of all evil. LOVE of money is the root of all evil. And Jesus says what's more important than all of that is the love of GOD.

So, again, when we're talking about the tithe we're really talking about Jesus. Apply that truth to this passage:

"Will a man rob God? Yet ye have robbed me. But ye say, Wherein have we robbed thee? In tithes and offering. Ye are cursed with a curse: for ye have robbed me, even this whole nation. Bring ye all the tithes into the storehouse, that there may be meat in mine house, and prove me now herewith, saith the LORD of hosts, if I will not open you the windows of heaven, and pour you out a blessing, that there shall not be room enough to receive it. And I will rebuke the devourer for your sakes, and he shall not destroy the fruits of your ground; neither shall your vine cast her fruit before the time in the field, saith the LORD of hosts. And all nations shall call you blessed: for ye shall be a delightsome land, saith the LORD of hosts."

Ok. So we're not talking about giving money, but we're talking about Jesus. That makes this passage profound and powerful. Bring Jesus into the storehouse. Hmmm. What's the storehouse? WE ARE!!!

When we bring Jesus--who is already in us--into us, when we set our affections on Him, there will be meat in the house. Lamb's meat. We will be able to feast on Lamb and we will not go hungry.

When we bring Jesus into us, the Lord will prove Himself in us. Now this is key: It doesn't say God will open up the windows of heaven FOR us. It says God will open up US, the windows of heaven. WE are the windows of heaven! Jesus, or heaven, is in us. And in order to get out of us, in order for heaven to touch earth, the window has to be opened. Then it doesn't say God will pour out FOR you a blessing. It says God will pour YOU out a blessing. You're the storehouse, and you're the window, and you're the blessing that is poured out!

Of course when I say you're the storehouse, and the window, and the blessing, I'm saying it with the understanding that as He is, so are we in this world. That's what bringing Jesus into the storehouse means. It's the identification. Jesus is the tithe, and the storehouse, and the window, and the blessing. And since He's in us... WE are the tithe, and the storehouse, and the window, and the blessing.

So when Jesus is brought into us, Jesus will be poured out of us. And this will rebuke the devourer. This will make us so full of what we've been filled with that nothing and no one can take what we have and who we are away from us.

When Jesus is brought into us, Jesus will be poured out of us. And this will make sure the fruit comes in its season. And this will make sure the vine will cast her fruit onto the branches. (We're about to really get into the Vine, and the branches, and the fruit in a minute.)

When Jesus is brought into us, Jesus will be poured out of us. And then all the nations will call us blessed. And we shall be a delightsome land. A Promised Land. Jesus.

Chapter 12

The Fruit

The fruit of the Spirit is love. Stop. I know it's popular to preach about all the different fruit of the Spirit, and we're going to look at the passage that this teaching comes from, but guys... the fruit--singular--of the Spirit is love. Trees don't produce more than one kind of fruit. Apple trees don't produce apples, oranges, and pears. A seed can only produce after its own kind. What's in a seed is what comes out of the tree.

Galatians 5:22-23, *"But the fruit of the Spirit is love, joy, peace, longsuffering, gentleness, goodness, faith, Meekness, temperance: against such there is no law."*

I know there's a long list of "fruit" there. But what if the fruit of the Spirit is love, and the rest of the list is describing love? Love is so simple, but so vast. God is love. Which means love is God. Which means if you think you completely understand love... you don't.

Job chapter 26 looks at some of the great and wonderful works of the Lord. And then in verse 14 in the NIV he sums it up like this, *"And these are but the outer fringe of his works; how faint the whisper we hear of him! Who then can understand the thunder of his power?"*

Now I have to preface this by saying that was before the cross. Before the cross we could see the things God did, such as creating the earth and the sea, and bringing rain and all of those things. Now, on this side of the cross we can actually see God Himself. We see Him in the face of Jesus. And we see the face of Jesus when we look in the mirror.

The mystery--Christ in you the hope of glory--is not a mystery concealed anymore, but a mystery revealed! Here's the question though: Who then can understand the thunder of His power?

Well, what is His power? Love!

What is the fruit of the Spirit? Love!

It's all about love. Jesus is love in a human body. Period.

So when we look at the fruit we think we are supposed to produce--we're not supposed to PRODUCE it at all, but more on that in a minute--we need to understand that it's not a big list of things to do. The fruit of the Spirit is love. And while love encompasses joy, peace, longsuffering, gentleness, goodness, faith, meekness and temperance, you can't do any of those things without love and think that it's the fruit of the Spirit.

Look at what the beginning of 1 Corinthians 13, "the love chapter," says: *"Though I speak with the tongues of men and of angels, and have not charity, I am become as sounding brass, or a tinkling cymbal. And though I have the gift of prophecy, and understand all mysteries, and all knowledge; and though I have all faith, so that I could remove mountains, and have not charity, I am nothing. And though I bestow all my goods to feed the poor, and though I give my body to be burned, and have not charity, it profiteth me nothing"* (1 Corinthians 13:1-3).

None of your actions mean anything without love. But love WILL direct all of your actions. We are not saved BY good works, but we are saved UNTO good works.

Interesting too that Paul says if he has faith to remove mountains, but doesn't have love, then he is nothing. Remember the mountain is Mount Sinai--the Law. So removing the Law without inserting grace, or love, simply leaves you lawless. But against the fruit of the Spirit there is no Law.

This echoes what Jesus said in Matthew 7:12, *"Therefore all things whatsoever ye would that men should do to you, do ye even so to them: for this is the law and the prophets."* And what the Bible says in Romans 13:10, *"Love worketh no ill to his neighbour: therefore love is the fulfilling of the law."*

And before we go any further, I'm NOT saying that love allows you to keep the Law. I'm NOT saying grace empowers you to be able to follow the 10 Commandments. There is a very distinct difference between law and grace. Romans 6:14 puts it like this, *"For sin shall not have dominion over you: for ye are not under the law, but under grace."* Two things to notice here: 1) you can't be under both Law and grace. 2) if you're under the law sin has dominion over you. Again, the only thing the Law can produce is lawbreakers.

So I'm not saying, "If you love you can keep the Law." In fact, love is its own law. A higher law than the Law of Moses. The perfect law of liberty!

Remember how we look into the mirror with an unveiled face (without the Law) and we see Jesus inside us and we are changed from glory to glory? Well, look at what James chapter 1 says when it picks up this thought:

"But be ye doers of the word, and not hearers only, deceiving your own selves. For if any be a hearer of the word, and not a doer, he is like unto a man beholding his natural face in a glass: For he beholdeth himself, and goeth his way, and straightway forgetteth what manner of man he was. But whoso looketh into the perfect law of liberty, and continueth therein, he being not a forgetful hearer, but a doer of the work, this man shall be blessed in his deed" (James 1:22-25).

Here's the deal, if you hear the Word (love, Jesus) and don't receive it, then you behold YOUR natural face in the glass. You start looking at the outside instead of the inside. And straightaway you forget what image you've been conformed into. You forget what manner of man you really are. That's what the Law does. It tells you what a sinner you are.

But if you look into the perfect law of liberty, and continue in that liberty (or grace) you are doer of the work. And what is the work of the New Covenant? Believing! Believing that you are who God says you are! Believing that God loves you!

Ok.

"Perfect," is 5046 in Strong's Greek Concordance and means, "complete, in various applications of labor, growth, mental, and moral character. Completeness: - of full age, man, perfect." The perfect man, Jesus. The complete, or finished, work.

"Law," is G3551 and means, "to parcel out, especially food or grazing to animals." The baby Jesus was laid in a manger, or a feeding trough. And He is the Shepherd that makes us lie down in green pastures.

"Liberty," is G1657 and means, "freedom." Look at John 8:31-36, *"Then said Jesus to those Jews which believed on him, If ye continue in my word, then ye are my disciples indeed; And ye shall know the truth, and the truth shall make you free. They answered him, We be Abraham's seed, and were never in bondage to any man: how sayest thou, Ye shall be made free? Jesus answered them, Verily, verily, I say unto you, Whosoever committeth sin is the servant of sin. And the servant abideth not in the house forever: but the Son abideth ever. If the Son therefore shall make you free, ye shall be free indeed."*

Freedom is freedom from sin. Freedom from bondage. Freedom from the Law, or the ministry of condemnation.

So let's put these three words together and what we see is the perfect law of liberty is the finished work, or the perfect man, parceling out freedom! It's a higher law and a more excellent way. It's not Law, but grace. Not bondage, but liberty.

2 Corinthians 3:17 says, *"Now the Lord is that Spirit: and where the Spirit of the Lord is, there is liberty."*

Galatians 5:13-14 says, *"For, brethren, ye have been called unto liberty; only use not liberty for an occasion to the flesh, but by love serve one another. For all the law is fulfilled in one word, even in this; Thou shalt love thy neighbour as thyself."*

So where the Spirit of the Lord is, there is liberty. But not liberty to be lawless... liberty to love! Sin and death is the bondage that we were freed from. Our liberty is not to give occasion to the flesh--or our old nature, or human effort--but to serve one another by love! Our freedom isn't to be selfish... it is freedom FROM being selfish! Our freedom isn't to be lawless, but to be elevated to a higher law!

The perfect law of liberty, which can also be defined as the new commandment Jesus gave--love one another as Jesus loves us--is the fruit of the Spirit. The fruit of the Spirit is love. Period. There's only one fruit on the Tree of Life

So how do we continue in this perfect law of liberty? By eating the fruit of the Spirit! Adam got all of humanity into trouble by eating of the wrong tree, eating the wrong fruit. Jesus came and gave us a whole new diet!

When we eat the fruit of the Spirit we begin to stop focusing on what we are doing for God, and instead focus on what He did for us and as us! We stop focusing so much on trying to love God though our human effort and instead we focus on simply receiving God's love.

Peter was so sure that he loved Jesus that he swore up and down that he would go with him, all the way to death. Then he denied Jesus three times. This is what happens when we're focused on ourselves-- even focused on ourselves trying to love God--we fail. Miserably.

But that's when God can really prove to us that it's not about us--or our failures--at all. Look at this passage in the book of John. This is one of the last things that Jesus did. John 21:15-17, *"So when they had dined,*

Jesus saith to Simon Peter, Simon, son of Jonas, lovest thou me more than these? He saith unto him, Yea, Lord; thou knowest that I love thee. He saith unto him, Feed my lambs. He saith to him again the second time, Simon, son of Jonas, lovest thou me? He saith unto him, Yea, Lord; thou knowest that I love thee. He saith unto him, Feed my sheep. He saith unto him the third time, Simon, son of Jonas, lovest thou me? Peter was grieved because he said unto him the third time, Lovest thou me? And he said unto him, Lord, thou knowest all things; thou knowest that I love thee. Jesus saith unto him, Feed my sheep."

See, Peter denied Jesus three times, so Jesus gave Peter three opportunities to proclaim Him. And not only for Peter to SAY that he loved Jesus, but for Peter to begin to see HOW to love Jesus. Jesus said, "If you love me, feed my sheep." What do we feed the sheep? The fruit of the Spirit!

This is the heart of God. I'm convinced that there are only two things in this universe that are important: God and people. And life is all about loving these two things. Loving God and loving people. Loving God BY loving people.

But we can't give what we don't have. 1 John 4:19 says, *"We love him, because he first loved us."* We can't love until we understand that we are loved. Love flows from the source, which is God. Without God there is no love. Without the vine there is no fruit.

We can't give the fruit of the Spirit--love--until we first eat of the fruit of the Spirit. That's why, once again, the way love is described in 1 Corinthians 13 and other places isn't a list of things for us to do in order to love. It's a personality profile of Jesus. The Bible doesn't teach us how to love. It teaches us how to BE loved.

It's not until we see God as He truly is--as love--that we can identify with Him as He truly is. A verse like 1 John 4:17, *"Herein is our love made perfect, that we may have boldness in the day of judgment: because as he is, so are we in this world,"* doesn't mean a whole lot unless we know how He is!

The middle verse between our love being made perfect, and the truth that we love God because He first loved us, verse 18, says, *"There is no fear in love; but perfect love casteth out fear: because fear hath torment. He that feareth is not made perfect in love."* And it might sound like we're back to putting yokes on people: If you fear, then you're obviously not made perfect in love. But that's not it.

The fear, way back in the garden of Eden, was that man wasn't good enough to be loved. That we needed to perform in order to earn God's love. That it took knowledge of good and evil so that we could stop doing evil and start doing good, and thereby be accepted.

That's the problem with eating from the wrong tree though: It doesn't produce life. It produces death. It focuses on Law, not relationship. It focuses on fear--behaving a certain way or else--rather than love.

As far as the Law goes, I'm convinced that there are two types of people. There are people who know that they are the righteousness of God in Christ... and they don't need a set of external rules because they are led by the Holy Spirit. And there are people who don't know, or care, that they are the righteousness of God in Christ... and they aren't going to follow the Law anyway. So no matter who you are, the Law only serves its purpose--not by getting you to follow it--but by bringing you to Christ. Once it does that, it's done its job.

Your EPIC destiny is not to follow a bunch of rules. It is to be conformed into the image of Christ. And it has already been fulfilled. Now, by eating the fruit of the Spirit, which is love, we do our part, which is finding out what the image that we have been conformed into looks like.

This is straight out of Six Steps to the Throne, but I guess I'm going to keep saying it until somebody believes it:

"Let me link together two verses: Proverbs 25:2, *"It is the glory of God to conceal a thing: but the honour of kings is to search out a matter,"* and Colossians 3:3, *"For ye are dead, and your life is hid with Christ in God."* God hid your life—your new resurrection life, your REAL life—with Christ in Himself. That is His glory. It's our honor (and our responsibility) to search it out. As we find Jesus, we find ourselves. As we understand who He is, we understand who we are."

See, it's not about figuring out how to love. It's not about conforming to any specific behaviors. It's about figuring out that we ARE loved. It's about figuring out that we HAVE BEEN conformed, not to behavior, but to the image of Jesus!

And the way we find our life--Jesus' life in us--is by eating the fruit of the Spirit. By eating Lamb. By eating bread and drinking wine.

Adam ate from the wrong tree and got us into a whole mess of trouble with sin and death. Jesus came AS the Tree of Life and offered Himself both for us and to us.

The old saying, "You are what you eat," has a lot of truth to it. Especially spiritually speaking. If you eat from the tree of death, you're going to be the walking dead. And not because God is mad at you, but because a seed can only produce after its own kind. That's not punishment. That's a law of nature that God set up a long, long time ago.

It's the same principle behind outer darkness. Jesus uses that term three times in the King James Bible: Matthew 8:12, Matthew 22:13, and Matthew 25:30. And every time it is accompanied by weeping and gnashing of teeth. Sounds like a pretty terrible punishment, right?

Except Jesus was talking about people who rejected Him. And He wasn't talking about punishment at all. He was simply saying, "If you reject the light, what is left but darkness?" And if you're in the darkness, what else would you do but stumble around and weep and wail and gnash your teeth?

Jesus came to give us something to believe in. He came to give us fruit from the Tree of Life. He came to show us what God looks like, so that we could understand what WE look like now that God lives in us.

Man's appetite has always been for love. More than anything else, we want to be loved. That's why Adam did what he did with the tree of death. He didn't have the Holy Spirit so he couldn't receive God's love. But he was desperate for God's love. So if he had to earn it... well, he'd earn it.

Adam's problem was a problem of faith. He didn't believe that God could love him apart from his actions. He tied what he did with how God would relate to him. "If I behave then I'll be loved."

This was never the case though. God didn't tell Adam, "If you sin I'll punish you." He said, "If you eat from the tree of death, you'll die." And friends, that just makes sense. That's not punishment. That's common sense.

See, according to Genesis 3:7, *"And they heard the voice of the LORD God walking in the garden in the cool of the day: and Adam and his wife hid themselves from the presence of the LORD God amongst the trees of the garden."* Adam THOUGHT God was mad at him, so he hid from God's presence. Adam was afraid of God.

But perfect love casts out fear.

If we turn AWAY from judging ourselves by our actions, and thinking that the way we see ourselves is the way God sees us, then we will be able to turn TO a loving heavenly Father who would rather die than be without us. If we can let God change our diet... if we stop eating--or focusing on--good and evil, and start eating--or focusing on--God's love for us, we will be able to see what the image is that we have been conformed to.

There's only one fruit on the Tree of Life. And it is love. There is only one thing that brings and sustains life. And it is love.

We love God because He first loved us. And we are ABLE to love only because God loves us. Ephesians 5:1-2 in the Message Bible, *"Watch what God does, and then you do it, like children who learn proper behavior from their parents. Mostly what God does is love you.*

Keep company with him and learn a life of love. Observe how Christ loved us. His love was not cautious but extravagant. He didn't love in order to get something from us but to give everything of himself to us. Love like that."

Only through receiving God's love can we release God's love. Jesus taught Peter HOW to love when He told Peter to feed His sheep. And what do we feed them? The fruit from the Tree of Life. The fruit of the Spirit. The fruit that we ourselves feast on, and are full of.

But, as we're going to see next chapter, we CANNOT produce this fruit. That's ok though, because we're not supposed to. We're simply supposed to bear this fruit.

Chapter 13

Bearing Fruit

A tree doesn't try really hard to produce fruit. It produces fruit because it's a tree. The work was done when the seed was planted. Everything else flows naturally from there.

Here's the key though: We are not the tree. Jesus is the tree. We are the branches. And God the Father is the husbandman who did the work of planting the seed, and does the work of pruning the branches.

John 15:1-9, *"I am the true vine, and my Father is the husbandman. Every branch in me that beareth not fruit he taketh away: and every branch that beareth fruit, he purgeth it, that it may bring forth more fruit. Now ye are clean through the word which I have spoken unto you. Abide in me, and I in you. As the branch cannot bear fruit of itself, except it abide in the vine; no more can ye, except ye abide in me. I am the vine, ye are the branches: He that abideth in me, and I in him, the same bringeth forth much fruit: for without me ye can do nothing. If a man abide not in me, he is cast forth as a branch, and is withered; and men gather them, and cast them into the fire, and they are burned. If ye abide in me, and my words abide in you, ye shall ask what ye will, and it shall be done unto you. Herein is my Father glorified, that ye bear much fruit; so shall ye be my disciples. As the Father hath loved me, so have I loved you: continue in my love."*

I feel like this is a popular passage, but I also feel like we use it a little bit incorrectly. I think we use it for the opposite of what it was intended for. This passage is NOT about Jesus warning us that if we don't produce fruit we'll go to hell. Not even a little bit.

Let's unwrap it. Jesus is the vine. He did all the work, and all the fruit production. Remember that the fruit (singular) of the Spirit is love. That's what Jesus produced. That's not what we're supposed to produce, and it's not something we can produce. God is love. That's where love comes from. Period. If it's not love it's not God.

We have to get rid of this mindset where we think we can try really hard to love, and if we love, then we'll be accepted by God. That's not how it works. In fact, that's labor and works. We love God because He first loved us (1 John 4:19). It flows from the source. A branch can't produce fruit.

Only one time in all of history did a branch produce fruit: *"And it came to pass, that on the morrow Moses went into the tabernacle of witness; and, behold, the rod of Aaron for the house of Levi was budded, and brought forth buds, and bloomed blossoms, and yielded almonds"* (Numbers 17:8). This was done for two reasons, 1) to show the people of Israel, who were rebelling against Aaron and Moses, that Aaron was God's chosen priest. 2) as a type and shadow of Jesus--the dead rod brought forth fruit. Jesus died in order to bring forth the harvest.

As a branch, or a rod, you can't do it. Jesus said, *"Abide in me, and I in you. As the branch cannot bear fruit of itself, except it abide in the vine; no more can ye, except ye abide in me"* (John 15:4). So this passage isn't about behaving a certain way. It's about understanding that love comes only from the source. Unless we're connected to the source, or the vine, then love cannot flow.

Amazingly, Jesus said in the verse right before that one, *"Now ye are clean through the word which I have spoken unto you."* He was talking about branches that don't bear fruit in verse two. Then in verse three He said we are clean. So... where's the scary part? Where's the punishment part? Where's the hellfire and brimstone part?

Jesus isn't talking about PEOPLE being burned. He's not talking about PEOPLE being pruned, or purged. He's talking about love. He's not talking about wicked people, He's talking about wickedness IN people!

He made us clean, but until we can see that truth, we're going to act like we're dirty. And while we're acting like we're dirty, we aren't bearing fruit. It's only through receiving the word that made us clean can we truly be who we are. Look, hurting people hurt people. But loved people love people. It's that simple.

Jesus was saying, "If there's anything in your life that doesn't line up with love, we're going to get rid of it. And if there's anything that does line up with love we're going to make sure it continues to develop and grow."

The fire is never for punishment. Ever. God is the fire. God is love. Love doesn't punish. Here's what love does, according to Proverbs 3:12, *"For whom the LORD loveth he correcteth; even as a father the son in whom he delighteth."* Love corrects, but it doesn't punish.

And when we're looking at this burning--or purifying--process, it's vital to understand that God is the husbandman. He is the Vinedresser, according to the Amplified Bible, or the Farmer, according to the Message Bible. So who purifies us? Who sanctifies us? Who makes us clean?

God!

We don't have to change. God changed us on the cross. The deal is not becoming more and more like God. The deal is God revealing to us that as He is, so are we in this world! The work of pruning, and the work of purifying, was all done on the cross. The work is finished.

What I'm trying to say is... you don't have to sanctify yourself. And in fact you can't, so trying is going to frustrate you and make you feel like a failure. Trying to produce fruit is going to frustrate you and make you feel like a failure. When it comes to love, you can't fake it 'til you make it. Because you'll never make it on your own.

We have to get out of this mindset of thinking, "What I'm doing is what matters." It's not about what you're doing. It's about what Jesus did on the cross! This, I'm convinced, is the repentance that we need. We have to shift our focus off of ourselves, and each other, and get it where it belongs: On Jesus!

Matthew 3:12 in the Message Bible says, *"He's going to clean house--make a clean sweep of your lives. He'll place everything true in its proper place before God; everything false he'll put out with the trash to be burned."* This is the purifying, and the pruning. And, again, look who does it: God!

You don't have to focus on the garbage, even to try to get rid of it. That's not your job. You are the branch, which is connected to the vine. You only have one job: believe that you're connected.

You are not supposed to clean up your life. And you can't. Jesus made you clean. You are not supposed to produce fruit. And you can't. Jesus produced the fruit.

You are supposed to BEAR fruit. John 15:8, *"Herein is my Father glorified, that ye bear much fruit; so shall ye be my disciples."*

This is so key. Because, again, the fruit is love. But if you're trying to produce love on your own... you're going to fail. If you think keeping the Law will glorify the Father... it won't. The way to be Jesus' disciple, the way to glorify God, the way to fulfill your EPIC destiny, is to bear much fruit.

The word, "bear," in John 15:8 is number 5342 in Strong's Greek Concordance and it simply means, "carry." A branch doesn't produce anything. It simply carries what the vine produced. So the fruit that we bear, or carry, is the love of God.

This should be our only mission in life: Carrying the love of God. Jesus said His new commandment was to love one another as He loves us. He is the love. He gives it (and Himself) to us, and we carry it. We live in it. We enjoy it. That's it.

We love God because He first loved us. We love God by loving each other. We love each other because God's love IN US allows us to! It's not, "fake it 'til you make it." It's, "I'm so full of God's love that I can't contain it!"

2 Corinthians 4:7, *"But we have this treasure in earthen vessels, that the excellency of the power may be of God, and not of us."*

Listen, we are the earthen vessel that God has hidden His treasure in. The treasure is Jesus. The treasure is love. We don't produce the treasure. We simply carry it. If we produced it, we could boast about it, and the excellency would be ours and not God's.

Ephesians 2:9 says it like this, *"Not of works, lest any man should boast."* And Psalm 44:8 tells us the only boasting we should do, *"In God we boast all the day long, and praise thy name for ever. Selah."*

Why is this important? Because according to Proverbs 16:18, *"Pride goeth before destruction, and a haughty spirit before a fall."* When we think it's all about us, we get into big trouble. When we judge ourselves, and each other, by our actions, and we think if we do good instead of evil, what we really find is that, *"...there is none righteous, no, not one"* (Romans 3:10). This is what Jesus was talking about when He said the branch can't do anything unless it's connected to the vine.

Let me link two passages together: Job 41:15-16, *"His scales are his pride, shut up together as with a close seal. One is so near to another, that no air can come between them,"* and Acts 9:17-18, *"And Ananias went his way, and entered into the house; and putting hands on him said, Brother Saul, the Lord, even Jesus, that appeared unto thee in the way as thou camest, hath sent me, that thou mightest receive thy sight, and be filled with the Holy Ghost. And immediately there fell from his eyes as it had been scales: and he received sight forthwith, and arose, and was baptized."*

Leviathan's scales are his pride. And they are so close together that the wind--the Holy Spirit--can't blow. What's inside can't get out. The incorruptible seed that was planted on the cross can't bring forth fruit because pride is holding it back. Trying to produce fruit actually stops one from bearing it!

But when Ananias, which means grace, entered the scene, everything changed. The scales that were blinding Saul--making him think his works and labor could produce the fruit of love--fell from his eyes. And He was filled with the Holy Ghost. He was finally able to be full of what he had been filled with. The Holy Spirit--our love receptor--finally had room to operate.

But here's the key: Saul was blinded by his pride. He was doing wrong because he thought it was right. I know there are a lot of well-intentioned people out there who preach the Law because they think keeping the Law will produce fruit. They're sincere, but they're sincerely wrong.

And I don't say this to anyone's shame, but instead to shine the light of Jesus so that we can see clearly. So that we can see that it is Jesus that produced the fruit because it is Jesus who IS the fruit! It's all about Him. All we do is carry Him. All we do is believe.

And here's the cool thing about being the branches on the Tree of Life: the branches are what reach out. The tree is up and down. It, like Jacob's ladder, allows things to come down from heaven to earth and vice versa. It is the vertical part of the cross. The branches are the horizontal part of the cross. The branches carry what the tree produces outward to those that need it!

See, the vine--or Jesus--has everything we need. Jesus IS everything we need. But it's the branches that deliver the fruit to the world around it. You don't pick fruit off a tree. You pick fruit off a tree BRANCH.

We carry God's love out into the world. We don't produce the fruit, but we take it to those who are hungry for it. Remember, you are what you eat. And if you don't know that there's anything but the fruit of the tree of death, you'll never be able to change your diet. Jesus came to show us a more excellent way. And now that we know the Way (Jesus), we can show it (Him) to others!

Jesus said He is the light of the world. And then He said WE are the light of the world. It's all one light. He shines in us. His love in us is the fruit that we bear!

So how do we bear this fruit? How do we carry the love of Jesus?

Proverbs 18:20-21 gives us vital insight, *"A man's belly shall be satisfied with the fruit of his mouth; and with the increase of his lips shall he be filled. Death and life are in the power of the tongue: and they that love it shall eat the fruit thereof."*

What we say is so important. Because what we say is really what we believe. What's in us is what comes out of us. We may KNOW the truth, but it's not until we start to believe what we know that what's inside of us begins to work its way out of us. Basically, when we see it, we'll believe it. And when we believe it, we'll say it. And when we say it, we'll BE it!

Let me say it another way, *"Let the redeemed of the LORD say so, whom he hath redeemed from the hand of the enemy"* (Psalm 107:2).

And another way, *"For with the heart man believeth unto righteousness; and with the mouth confession is made unto salvation."*

Ecclesiastes 8:4 says, *"Where the word of a king is, there is power."* The King of kings lives in us. That makes us kings. That means our words have power. Death and life are in the power of our tongue. And I don't think it's any accident that death is listed before life.

I quoted Romans 3:10, but let's look at the verses that follow it. *"As it is written, There is none righteous, no, not one: There is none that understandeth, there is none that seeketh after God. They are all gone out of the way, they are together become unprofitable; there is none that doeth good, no, not one. Their throat is an open sepulchre; with their tongues they have used deceit; the poison of asps is under their lips: Whose mouth is full of cursing and bitterness"* (Romans 3:10-13).

First things first though: Who is this passage talking about? Adam! Man! The corruptible seed! The tree of death! This passage describes the fruit of the wrong tree! And the fruit goes in the mouth (in the natural) and comes out of the mouth (in the spiritual).

If you're carrying anything other than the fruit of the Spirit, it's going to come out when you talk, and it's going to come out when you walk. It's going to come out in what you say and what you do. You are what you eat. And you can't give what you don't have.

So we carry the fruit by eating it--by dwelling in God's love for us, and by living in that love--and we carry it by proclaiming it. I remember a time when I was at work, and a co-worker asked me why I was always in a good mood. We literally did the same job, at the same place, day after day. So what was the difference between me and him? How come I could smile all day long?

Here's what I told him: "Bro, I'm always in a good mood because Jesus loves me."

See, I didn't have to cram Bible verses down his throat. And if I had, he probably would have choked on them. I didn't have to convince him that my way was right and his way was wrong. If you attack people, they're not going to want what you have, they're going to want to get away from you. All I had to do was bear the fruit.

And when I carried God's love for me, those around me saw it. And when they saw it, and wanted it--whatever it was--then there was an opportunity for me to speak about it. An opportunity for me to share the fruit!

Believing is the first part of our response to God. And we're going to get into that in a couple of chapters. Because it's by grace THROUGH FAITH. But confession is the next part. Confession is how you literally put your money where your mouth is. Or put your mouth where your heart is.

Remember how God told Moses to speak to the Rock? It's not about us doing any work, or smiting the Rock. The Rock was smitten on the cross. It's about us speaking to--or about--the Rock. And here's a key that should make it easy for you to speak about it, or confess it: Just think about the things in life that you love. Those are the things you talk about naturally. I can't shut up about my son, Logan, because I love the stuffing out of him. He's my pride and joy. He's the apple of my eye.

In the exact same way we are God's pride and joy! We are the apple of His eye! We don't have to do anything but just speak about His goodness. And we CAN speak about His goodness because He shows it to us! We don't have to make stuff up to make God look good. He looks good all by Himself.

It's the fruit that we eat that allows us to share the same fruit. And it's so good that we don't have to force ourselves to eat it, or to share it! Psalm 34:8 says it like this, *"O taste and see that the LORD is good: blessed is the man that trusteth in him."* God's not afraid of you putting Him to the test. He is the answer to the test!

I'm saying, just live out of your experience with God. Just live in His love for you and you'll be full of praise for how good that love is! That's what Jesus was saying in John 15:7, *"If ye abide in me, and my words abide in you, ye shall ask what ye will, and it shall be done unto you."*

First we abide, then we ask (or speak). First we believe, then we confess. We begin to see what's inside us, and then it begins to come out of us!

Let me end this chapter by setting up the next chapter. In the true paradise of God, New Jerusalem, there is a river of life that proceeds out of the throne of God and the Lamb. This river flows out of the Tree of Life, and out of the street of the city.

We are New Jerusalem. We are the branches of the Tree of Life. We carry the fruit of the Spirit. And we flow in the river of life!

Chapter 14

The River of Life

Revelation 22:1-5, *"And he shewed me a pure river of water of life, clear as crystal, proceeding out of the throne of God and of the Lamb. In the midst of the street of it, and on either side of the river, was there the tree of life, which bare twelve manner of fruits, and yielded her fruit every month: and the leaves of the tree were for the healing of the nations. And there shall be no more curse: but the throne of God and of the Lamb shall be in it; and his servants shall serve him: And they shall see his face; and his name shall be in their foreheads. And there shall be no night there; and they need no candle, neither light of the sun; for the Lord God giveth them light: and they shall reign for ever and ever."*

Love feeds on love. God, who is a consuming fire, consumes everything that isn't Him, and everything that IS Him spreads like wildfire. The River of Life feeds the Tree of Life, but it also flows FROM the Tree of Life.

New Jerusalem, the true paradise of God, has a street called straight. It has a highway called holiness. It has one Way, and His name is Jesus. Jesus is the street, and the Tree, and the River. It's all Jesus.

And listen, I know this passage speaks of twelve manner of fruit. But that's like saying there are twelve different kinds of apples. Love is the fruit, but it encompasses things like joy, peace, longsuffering, etc. Those are the different manners of the fruit--the different manifestations of love.

So we're still on track. We bear the fruit, which is love. We were planted in corruption and harvested in incorruption. We have been given the Holy Spirit, our love receptor, so that we can receive and release God's love. We feast on it, and we share it. But it's not hard work, it's flowing in the River!

Look at John 7:37-38, *"In the last day, that great day of the feast, Jesus stood and cried, saying, If any man thirst, let him come unto me, and drink. He that believeth on me, as the scripture hath said, out of his belly shall flow rivers of living water."* In the Message Bible it reads, *"On the final and climactic day of the Feast, Jesus took his stand. He cried out, "If anyone thirsts, let him come to me and drink. Rivers of living water will brim and spill out of the depths of anyone who believes in me this way, just as the Scripture says."*

So here's the key: Not only do we flow IN the River... the River flows OUT of us! Our passage in Revelation reveals that the River proceeds out of the throne of God and of the Lamb. We are in the Throne because the Throne is in us! You can't give what you don't have. You have to first drink of the River--and get it in you--by believing, before you can be so full that it brims and spills out of you. You have to receive before you can release.

In Matthew 5:6 Jesus says, *"Blessed are those who hunger and thirst after righteousness: for they shall be filled."* But we have to remember who Jesus was talking about. He wasn't telling us to hunger and thirst after righteousness. He was talking about Himself. HE hungered and thirsted after righteousness, and He was filled with the Holy Spirit.

Flowing in the River, and carrying the fruit of the Spirit, doesn't come from trying really hard. It doesn't come from us at all. It comes from the source. The first part of Song of Solomon chapter one verse four says, *"Draw me, we will run after thee."*

This is the way God's economy works. He draws us, and because of this drawing, we run after Him. Coming to God was never man's idea.

Man's idea was running away from God because he thought God was angry.

God draws us to Himself by shining the light and showing us who He really is. Look at what Philippians 2:13 says in the Amplified Bible, *"[Not in your own strength] for it is God Who is all the while effectually at work in you [energizing and creating in you the power and desire], both to will and to work for His good pleasure and satisfaction and delight."* It's God inside us that creates a desire to bear fruit, and it's God inside us that gives us the fruit, and it's God inside us that gives us the ability to bear the fruit!

We flow, because we're in the River. We rest, because God did all the work! It all flows from the source.

Now watch this: John 12:32-33, *"And I, if I be lifted up from the earth, will draw all men unto me. This he said, signifying what death he should die."*

On the cross Jesus drew us all to Himself! The drawing is a done deal. The desire for God has been placed inside us, and the love receptor allows us to have this desire fulfilled! I'm convinced that before the cross all people were born with a God-shaped hole inside them. Then, on the cross, that hole was filled.

Man was born dark, and formless, and void. Then God said, "Let there be light." Our EPIC destiny was fulfilled on the cross! We didn't know who we were, or who God was. Then Jesus entered the scene, and everything became clear. We realized that we were made in His image, and we could finally see what that image is!

Jesus hungered and thirsted after righteousness, and He was filled. Then He filled US with Himself! He drew us all into Himself and put His Spirit in all of us. He transformed us from sinner (unbeliever) to saint (believer) by giving us something to believe in!

The River is inside of us, and when we believe that truth it flows out of us. We don't have to make the River flow, because it is so powerful it can only be held back by unbelief. The only way the River DOESN'T flow out of you is if you don't believe it's IN you. And the reason for that is because if you don't believe it's in you, you'll try to get it. God put the want in us. So if you have the want, but don't believe you have what you want... then you won't be able to receive and enjoy what you have!

Man is thirsty. Man always wants something better. The grass always looks greener on the other side. And it always looks greener, because it always looks like it's been watered. The Tree of Life is watered by the River of Life.

John 4:13-14 says it like this, *"Jesus answered and said unto her, Whosoever drinketh of this water shall thirst again: But whosoever drinketh of the water that I shall give him shall never thirst; but the water that I shall give him shall be in him a well of water springing up into everlasting life."*

There was a woman at the well of Jacob, and there was Jesus. Jesus was a well that was sitting on a well. He knew where people went when they were thirsty. The well of Jacob. Jacob is a type and shadow of Jesus, but Jacob used human effort to get everything he could get. He was a swindler, and a con artist. He stepped on people to get to the top.

That's how we think we get ahead. We think if we can dig our own well we can drink whenever we want and quench our thirst. Build up a kingdom for ourselves, and live happily ever after. But Jesus knew the folly of this system. He said, "Whoever drinks of THIS water shall thirst again."

Drinking from the well of Jacob is the same as eating from the tree of death. It doesn't satisfy. It might refresh us for a minute, but we'll be thirsty again before too long. This is the same trap religion, and the Law, keeps us bound in. We might be able to behave for a little while, but it's not true righteousness. We are trying to conform to an image of Jesus, but really we are just wearing ourselves out. We aren't flowing in the River... we're trying to swim upstream.

Jesus said if we drink the right water it'll transform us into a well of the same water! You are what you eat (and drink). God's love transforms us into God's love! See, the cross did NOT transform us into something God could love. God always loved us. What the cross did was transform us into something that could RECEIVE God's love!

So the River flows out of the well, or out of the Throne. Let's see what the Bible has to say about the well.

Proverbs 10:11, *"The mouth of a righteous man is a well of life: but violence covereth the mouth of the wicked."*

Proverbs 18:4, *"The words of a man's mouth are as deep waters, and the wellspring of wisdom as a flowing brook."*

Isaiah 12:3, *"Therefore with joy shall ye draw water out of the wells of salvation."*

Once again we see how powerful our words are. The world says, "Actions speak louder than words," but I'm convinced there's nothing louder, or more powerful, than the Word of God. And according to John chapter one, the Word of God is Jesus. When God spoke He said, "Let there be light." He introduced Jesus into the life, or circumstance, or situation. He gave us something to believe in. He gave us the power to will and to do.

He gave us the power to speak to Rock. He gave us the power to let what's in us flow out of us. And really, what's in us flows out of us naturally, when we understand that we are full to overflowing!

Isaiah gives us this insight, "Therefore with JOY shall ye draw water out of the wells of salvation." It's not complaining to God. It's not treating God like a genie that grants us wishes. It's not telling God how big the storm is. It's telling the storm how big God is! It's the JOY of the Lord that is our strength. It's His love in us--the Holy Spirit--that gives us righteousness, peace, and JOY.

We flow in the River by enjoying the ride. We don't try to get anywhere, because we know the truth that we're already where we need to be. Speaking about God like a ball and chain that you have to drag around isn't drawing living water out of the wells of salvation.

Psalm 37:4 says, *"Delight thyself also in the LORD; and he shall give thee the desires of thine heart."*

This can sound like a formula for getting what you want. IF I delight myself in the Lord THEN I get the desires of my heart. But that's not it at all. Because when you truly delight yourself in the Lord, you understand that His heart IS your heart. And when you understand whose heart it is, you understand whose desire it is.

I once preached a sermon about the New Creation's appetite. And the whole time I was preparing the sermon I was convinced I was going to tell everybody how grace changes your appetite. How when you understand that God loves you, you won't want all the garbage you used to want. And, man, I was fired up. I thought, "This'll preach!"

But the day before I was going to preach this message, God checked me. He told me one of the most important truths in the universe. Ready?

Grace doesn't change man's appetite. Grace allows man's appetite to be satisfied.

God told me, "Man's appetite is the same as it ever was, and it's the same as it always will be." I said, "Well what's man's appetite then?" God said, "To be loved."

Ahhh! That blew up a lot of my preconceived notions. That blew up a lot of my thoughts about people, and why they do what they do. But it also made perfect sense.

Eve ate from the tree of knowledge of good and evil, not because she wanted to disobey God, but because she wanted to be loved, and she thought she had to earn it. She had good intentions, but didn't know that she couldn't earn what was freely given. She was deceived. Tricked.

She was looking for love in all the wrong places.

And this is where most of humanity is. Remember that God-shaped hole we talked about earlier? That's the desire--no, the NEED--for love. And only God can fill it, because God IS love. If it ain't love it ain't God. And if it ain't God it ain't love.

We get into so much trouble because we try to fill this God-shaped love hole on our own. Solomon wrote a whole book in the Bible about how life under the sun is nothing but vanity. He tried his best to fill that hole inside him with anything and everything. But nothing fit. Nothing satisfied. He drank the world's water and got thirsty again. He ate from the tree of death and found no life in it.

Here's the difference though: Life UNDER the sun... or Life IN the Son!

The Apostle Paul said it like this, *"What fruit had ye then in those things whereof ye are now ashamed? for the end of those things is death. But now being made free from sin, and become servants to God, ye have your fruit unto holiness, and the end everlasting life"* (Romans 6:21-22).

We built up a lot of sin, and iniquity, and condemnation, and shame when we were looking for love in all the wrong places. We were trying to earn something that can't be earned. We were trying to earn a gift. And the end of all of that sin (or unbelief) and all of that human effort... is death. There is no life under the sun. There is only life IN the Son!

When Adam and Eve were first joined together in marriage they were naked and not ashamed. It wasn't until they got on the wrong diet that they became ashamed of their nakedness. It wasn't until they stopped flowing and started trying to swim... wasn't until they stopped resting and started working... that things got messed up.

We already quoted Romans 10:10 regarding confession. Here's Romans 10:11, *"For the scripture saith, whosoever believeth on him shall not be ashamed."*

When we take the focus off of us, and put it on Jesus where it belongs, we stop being ashamed. We let what's really in us--the Holy Spirit, the love of God--bubble up out of us. And it comes out of the well, or our mouths.

Romans 1:16 declares, *"For I am not ashamed of the gospel of Christ: for it is the power of God unto salvation to every one that believeth; to the Jew first, and also to the Greek."*

The things we were ashamed of were our own efforts. Believing that we needed to earn God's love, and believing that we COULD earn God's love. That's shameful, because it's a lie. And it's painful, because it's like banging your head against the wall. You're not going to accomplish anything, you're only going to get a headache.

God's love flows into us so that it can flow out of us. That's the River. It feeds the Tree of Life and it runs out of the Tree of Life. We are wells of salvation, and the love bubbles out through our mouths. We bear the fruit by flowing in the River.

One more thought on our words. Revelation 12:11 says, *"And they overcame him by the blood of the Lamb, and by the word of their testimony; and they loved not their lives unto the death."*

First things first: the book of Revelation is about the cross. It's not in your future, it's in your past. Hence the past tense. They OVERCAME. Not, "they will overcome." We are overcomers because Jesus overcame. Jesus told us to be of good cheer because He has overcome the world. He did the overcoming on the cross. We don't need to overcome, or to conquer. Jesus did the overcoming, and the conquering. We are MORE than conquerors in Him.

Secondly, we overCAME by the blood of the Lamb and the WORD of our testimony. But since words are so important... what is the

WORD of our testimony? I put it in all caps because the WORD of our testimony is Jesus! He is the Word!

We didn't overcome by anything we did, we overcame by everything He did! And we appropriate who Jesus is (and who we are, the image that we are conformed into), not by talking about us but by talking about Him!

Jesus said, *"It is the spirit that quickeneth; the flesh profiteth nothing: the words that I speak unto you, they are spirit, and they are life"* (John 6:63).

The Word that Jesus spoke to us... is Jesus. He is the Word. He is the Spirit, and He is the Life. It's all Jesus.

So when we speak Jesus, we are bearing the fruit. We are carrying love to those that desperately need it. When we speak Jesus it's not about us, and we can flow in the River that proceeds out of the Throne of God and the Lamb.

It's all Jesus. Everything is working together, and feeding on itself, and expanding... and growing. And that growing process, that maturation process, is a lot of what grace is all about.

Chapter 15

Grace to Grow

Grace to grow. It hit me in the heart, right between the eyes. It explains grace in such a simple, powerful way. Grace allows us to mess up and not be thrown away. It allows us to fail, but not be a failure. It allows us to fall when we're learning to walk. The Law demands... but grace empowers.

Let's bring this back to the seed. I heard a good friend preach this one time and it made perfect sense: You don't plant a seed, wait two seconds, and then dig it up. You give the seed time to mature, and grow.

It's one thing for me to tell you that you're the righteousness of God in Christ Jesus. But it's another thing for you to know what the righteousness of God in Christ Jesus is. And it's ANOTHER thing for you to be what you now know you are. It's a process. Remember the excellent things? The three anointings of king David? 30 fold, 60 fold, 100 fold?

God doesn't expect us to hit the ground running. He's got all the time in the world (literally) to help us grow into what we are. To help us see the image the we have been conformed into. This, in fact, is the Holy Spirit's job. It leads us into all truth. John 16:13 bears this out, *"Howbeit when he, the Spirit of truth, is come, he will guide you into all truth: for he shall not speak of himself; but whatsoever he shall hear, that shall he speak: and he will shew you things to come."*

What the Spirit hears is the Word of God. So what the Spirit speaks is the Word of God. That's what all truth is: God loves you. And that's what grace does: it empowers you to receive this love apart from your actions.

I've heard two definitions of grace, and they both apply. Grace is:

The unmerited favor of God.

The enabling power of God.

Mercy is us not getting what we deserve, and grace is us getting what we don't deserve. 2 Corinthians 8:9 defines grace like this, *"For ye know the grace of our Lord Jesus Christ, that, though he was rich, yet for your sakes he became poor, that ye through his poverty might be rich."*

Grace is God's Riches At Christ's Expense. It is us getting it all because Jesus did it all. It is literally Jesus becoming sin so we could become the righteousness of God. It's the great exchange that happened at the cross. It's Jesus dying both for us and as us so that we can live both for Him and as Him!

But grace is so much more than that.

Grace is what empowers us to be who we are. Grace is what allows us to BE perfect, even as we figure out what it means to be perfect. The Law demands that you act perfect. But it doesn't empower you to do so. Grace is the perfect One living His life inside you, which empowers you to simply be who you are.

Guys, we're human BEINGS not human DOINGS. It's not about your actions. It's about your heart. It's not about what you do. It's about who you are.

Rest is about being, not doing. And the upside-down backwards way of the Kingdom goes like this: If you do, you'll never be. But if you be, you'll do naturally. We are not saved BY good works. We're saved

UNTO good works. *"For by grace are ye saved through faith; and that not of yourselves: it is the gift of God"* (Ephesians 2:8).

We are saved by grace. But here's something I want to make really really clear: We are NOT sinners saved by grace. We WERE sinners before the cross. Then we were saved by grace. Now we're not sinners anymore.

That's what grace means. It means we can now begin to be who we REALLY are. And if you've read Identity Crisis you know we're not Adam. We're Jesus. Grace saved us from all of the sin, and death, and bondage that we were trapped in. It is the unmerited favor of God.

Romans 5:19 says, *"For as by one man's disobedience many were made sinners, so by the obedience of one shall many be made righteous."* I like this verse even better in the Weymouth New Testament, *"For as through the disobedience of the one individual the mass of mankind were constituted sinners, so also through the obedience of the One the mass of mankind will be constituted righteous."* Because Adam's sin didn't make "many" sinners. It made everybody sinners. And by the same token Jesus' obedience didn't make "many" righteous. It made everybody righteous.

The difference between a believer and an unbeliever isn't that one is saved and one is damned. The difference is that one is found and one is lost. Lost means you don't know who you are or where you are. Lost means you don't know that you're righteous. I'm convinced that either the cross changed everything, or it didn't change anything. I'm convinced that the Messianic Rebirth of the World--when Jesus remade the world in His image--applied to everything and everybody.

1 John 2:2 says, *"And he is the propitiation for our sins: and not for ours only, but also for the sins of the whole world."* John 1:29 says, *"The next day John seeth Jesus coming unto him, and saith, Behold the Lamb of God, which taketh away the sin of the world."*

The cross is so much bigger than we make it out to be. Grace is so much bigger than we LET it be.

Grace is God's unmerited favor on everybody. It is also the enabling power of God. It is God, remember, that works both to will and to do in us for His good pleasure. It is God who draws us (and on the cross DREW us) to Himself.

God's grace is what allows us to be who we are, one step at a time. It is what allows the incorruptible seed to grow into the Holy thing that is Jesus! This is exactly what happened with Mary.

Luke 1:28-31, *"And the angel came in unto her, and said, Hail, thou that art highly favored, the Lord is with thee: blessed art thou among women. And when she saw him, she was troubled at his saying, and cast in her mind what manner of salutation this should be. And the angel said unto her, Fear not, Mary: for thou hast found favour with God. And, behold, thou shalt conceive in thy womb, and bring forth a son, and shalt call his name Jesus."*

Mary found favor with God. She found grace in the same place that Noah found it: in the eyes of the Lord. And this favor, this grace, empowered her to bring forth Jesus. He was planted in her by the Holy Spirit, and by grace (through faith) He came forth out of her! But Jesus didn't pop out immediately. He took nine months to grow from a seed into a harvest. And then He took another thirty years to grow before He began His ministry.

Speaking of Jesus, Hebrews 5:8-9 says, *"Though he were a Son, yet learned he obedience by the things which he suffered; And being made perfect, he became the author of eternal salvation unto all them that obey him."* Jesus learned obedience. And He BECAME perfect. This is key--perfection is not about never making a mistake. It's not about your actions. The phrase, "being made perfect," is number 5048 in Strong's Greek Concordance and it means, "to complete." It speaks of maturity, not of never messing up.

150

Jesus spoke of His own perfection in Luke 13:32, *"And he said unto them, Go ye, and tell that fox, Behold, I cast out devils, and I do cures today and to morrow, and the third day I shall be perfect."*

The third day, or the resurrection, brought forth the New Man. It is when we became complete in Him. And make no mistake, we ARE complete in Him. Colossians 2:10 says it explicitly, *"And ye are complete in him, which is the head of all principality and power."* The Amplified Bible reads, *"And you are in Him, made full and having come to fullness of life [in Christ you too are filled with the Godhead--Father, Son and Holy Spirit--and reach full spiritual stature]. And He is the Head of all rule and authority [of every angelic principality and power]."*

See, Jesus' perfection IS our perfection. We are complete in Him, because He is complete, and He is in us. We don't grow into something we aren't. We grow into what we are! We grow in our completeness as we are filled with what we are full of. As we understand the image that we have been conformed into.

The Message Bible says it like this, *"When you come to him, that fullness comes together for you, too. His power extends over everything."* His power, or His grace, extends over everything. Grace swallows up sin in the same way that love swallows up fear and life swallows up death and light swallows up darkness!

We think if we sin, we fall from grace. But the fact of the matter is... sin, or unbelief, loses to grace every time. Paul said, *"Moreover the law entered, that the offence might abound. But where sin abounded, grace did much more abound."* And listen--this verse is in the past tense. It's talking about Jesus and it's talking about the cross. Sin abounded until the cross. And then grace much more abounded.

Sin isn't the issue. Life is the issue. Proverbs 4:23 says, *"Keep thy heart with all diligence; for out of it are the issues of life."* The heart of the matter is the heart. Not sin.

In fact, the only way we can fall from grace is by putting ourselves back up under the Law. Galatians 5:4, *"Christ is become of no effect unto you, whosoever of you are justified by the law; ye are fallen from grace."*

Falling from grace isn't messing up. Grace allows you to mess up. The Law doesn't allow you to mess up. If you fall from grace, it's because you've put yourself back up under the Law. If you're justified by the Law, then there's no room for grace. But there's plenty of room for sin. Because, *"The sting of death is sin; and the strength of sin is the law"* (1 Corinthians 15:56).

Romans 3:21, *"But now the righteousness of God without the law is manifested, being witnessed by the law and the prophets."*

We are the righteousness of God WITHOUT THE LAW. And this is because of grace. In fact, *"...sin shall not have dominion over you: for ye are not under the law, but under grace"* (Romans 6:14). We are not under the Law. We are the righteousness of God without the Law. Not because of what we do, but because of what Jesus did on the cross! He saved us by grace, through faith.

We are complete in Him. The problem is that we don't know how complete He is, and because of that we don't know how complete we are. We don't know that the work is finished, so we keep trying to do the work. But guys, when we work God will rest. And when we rest God will work.

2 Peter 3:18 says it like this, *"But grow in grace, and in the knowledge of our Lord and Saviour Jesus Christ. To him be glory both now and for ever. Amen."*

Grace to grow is growing in grace! And we grow in grace by growing in the knowledge of Jesus! We find our identity in Him. We find our Promised Land in Him. We find our EPIC destiny... in Him!

I didn't know this when Jesus started writing Identity Crisis through me, but these books answer three of the most important questions man will ever ask: Who am I? Where am I? And why am I here?

Not very surprisingly, all three questions have one answer: Jesus.

Jesus saved us by grace, and He empowers us with grace. He gave us everything when He gave us Himself. God wanted the best for us so He gave the best (Jesus) to us!

2 Peter 1:2-3 says, *"Grace and peace be multiplied unto you through the knowledge of God, and of Jesus our Lord, According as his divine power hath given unto us all things that pertain unto life and godliness, through the knowledge of him that hath called us to glory and virtue."*

Let's try it this way: God has given us all things that pertain to life and godliness when He gave us grace and peace. He gave us everything when He gave us Himself. We already have it all. We just don't know what we have. We've already been conformed, we just don't know what we've been conformed into.

1 John 2:20 says, *"But ye have an unction from the Holy One, and ye know all things."* Let that sink in for a minute. We know all things. Because we have an unction from the Holy One. "Unction," is G5545 and it means, "special endowment of the Holy Spirit: - anointing."

The Amplified Bible says it like this, *"But you have been anointed by [you hold a sacred appointment from, you have been given an unction from] the Holy One, and you all know [the Truth] or you know all things."*

Knowing all things means knowing the Truth. Jesus is the Way, the Truth, and the Life. We know all things because we know Jesus. Because, *"...in him we live, and move, and have our being"* (Acts 17:28).

We know the Truth--all things--because we have been conformed into His image. He lives in us and we live in Him and there is no separation. We know the Truth because we ARE the Truth!

We just don't know what we know. And while the Holy Spirit (the Spirit of Truth) leads us into all truth--while we are finding out just what it is that we know--we have grace to grow. We are not learning how to be perfect. We are learning what it means that we ARE perfect!

Jesus said it like this, *"Be ye therefore perfect, even as your Father which is in heaven is perfect."* This wasn't mission impossible though. He wasn't saying, "Be perfect or you're in big trouble." He was telling us HOW to be perfect.

God told Abraham, *"...I am the Almighty God; walk before me, and be thou perfect"* (Genesis 17:1). Again, this wasn't a demand, it was an empowerment. That word, "before," is number 6440 in Strong's Hebrew Concordance and it means, "the face." God was literally telling Abraham (at that time Abram), "Walk facing me and you'll be perfect." Because what we behold... we become.

Psalm 37:37 says, *"Mark the perfect man, and behold the upright: for the end of that man is peace."* We find our perfection when we mark the perfect man. When we see Jesus--as He is--we will be Jesus. And the end of that man (Jesus) is peace. Grace and peace! All things pertaining to life and godliness!

The seed that was sown in corruption was harvested in incorruption. We are not who we always thought we were. We are not sinners saved by grace. We ARE conformed into the image of Jesus. Our EPIC destiny HAS been fulfilled.

But look at Philippians 3:12-15, *"Not as though I had already attained, either were already perfect: but I follow after, if that I may apprehend that for which I also am apprehended of Christ Jesus. Brethren, I count not myself to have apprehended: but this one thing I do, forgetting those things which are behind, and reaching forth unto those things which are before, I press toward the mark for the prize of the high calling of God in Christ Jesus. Let us therefore, as many as be perfect, be thus minded: and if in any thing ye be otherwise minded, God shall reveal even this unto you."*

First Paul says he's not perfect, but he's doing his best to apprehend what he's been apprehended of. And, of course, what he's been apprehended of is Jesus. But then he says, "Let us therefore, as many as are perfect, be thus minded." Seems like a contradiction, but it's not. What he's really saying is, "Let this mind of Christ that's in you... BE in you."

He's saying even though we're perfect, we need to figure out what that means. And we figure it out by letting God reveal it to us. By letting the Holy Spirit lead us into all truth. We know all things, but we need grace to figure out what we know.

We have been conformed, but we need to know what we've been conformed into. And before we figure out what we've been conformed into, we need to believe that we've been conformed. It's by grace through faith.

God's part is the Way of Grace. Our part is the Walk of Faith.

God did all the work, conforming us into the image of Jesus. All we have to do is respond.

Chapter 16

The Response

Up until the cross God had one song in His heart. Leviticus 26:12 declares it, but it is repeated all throughout the Old Testament. *"And I will walk among you, and will be your God, and ye shall be my people."* The Creator yearned for unity and relationship with His creation.

See, it was never about US getting to God. We didn't want to get to God. We thought He was mad and we wanted to get away from Him. Adam hid himself from the presence of God. It was never about us getting to God. It was about God getting to us.

1 John 4:10, *"Herein is love, not that we loved God, but that he loved us, and sent his Son to be the propitiation for our sins."*

"Propitiation," is number 2434 in Strong's Greek Concordance and it means, "atonement." The word, "atonement" is only used once in the King James Version of the Bible: Romans 5:11, *"And not only so, but we also joy in God through our Lord Jesus Christ, by whom we have now received the atonement."* The word, "atonement," is G2643 and it means, "exchange, that is, restoration to divine favor: - atonement, reconciliation."

Basically, our sin--or unbelief--separated us from God. It made us look at Him in the wrong way, and see ourselves in the wrong way. Our unbelief painted a picture of an angry God who only loved us if we were behaving ourselves. So Jesus, who knew no sin, became sin that we might become the righteousness of God in Christ Jesus.

Jesus took away the sin--or unbelief--of the world. He gave us something to believe in. He showed us the Father. He restored us to fellowship with a God that's not mad AT us, but mad ABOUT us!

God sowed His Son (and us in His Son) in corruption, so that we could be reaped in incorruption. God made a way to get to us. The way of Grace. His Son, Jesus, who is the Way, the Truth, and the Life.

When Jesus described Himself in John 14:6 He said, *"...I am the way, the truth, and the life: no man cometh unto the Father, but by me."* And we use this verse to force people to accept Jesus, or else. But look at what else Jesus said, *"No man can come to me, except the Father which hath sent me draw him: and I will raise him up at the last day"* (John 6:44).

So... No man comes to the Father except by Jesus. But... no man can come to Jesus except the Father draws him. Guys... it all comes from God. Man wasn't trying to get to God. God was drawing man to Himself! Jesus was lifted up on the cross and drew all men to Himself.

This is the way of grace.

Our response is the walk of faith.

Faith is what makes everything that is true... true for us. Faith is what connects us to the source--understanding, of course, that we ARE connected to it, whether we believe it or not. Believing it allows us to tap INTO the source that we've been connected to.

Now before we go any further, I want to make it as clear as I can: The whole deal, righteous, peace, joy, holiness... all of it... it all culminates in love. God is the source of love because He IS love. That's what we're connected to. Jesus is the vine and we are the branches. The fruit is love.

We tap into love because we're connected to the source of love. The Holy Spirit--the incorruptible seed--is our love receptor. It allows us to receive God's love. And receiving it allows us to release it. Eating the fruit allows us to bear the fruit. Drinking from the River allows us to flow in the River.

I said all that to say this: Your faith is what allows you believe that God loves you. That's what true faith is. Because when you believe that God loves you, everything else lines up in Divine Order.

We touched on this verse earlier, and I promised to pick it up in the faith chapter. Well, here we are. Galatians 2:20, *"I am crucified with Christ: nevertheless I live; yet not I, but Christ liveth in me: and the life which I now live in the flesh I live by the faith of the Son of God, who loved me, and gave himself for me."*

When Jesus was planted in corruption, so were you. When Jesus was raised in incorruption, so were you. This is when--and how--our EPIC destiny was fulfilled. We're alive, but it's not us living. It's Jesus living His life in and through us. That's what it means to be conformed into His image. It doesn't mean we act like Him. It means He acts in and through us!

And this part is so important, "the life which I now live in the flesh I live by the faith OF the Son of God." Not faith IN the Son of God. The faith OF the Son of God.

Remember how it's all about Jesus? Then it stands to reason that it's all about JESUS' faith. Jesus has perfect faith. Jesus never had an Identity Crisis. He knew who He was right from birth. He knew no sin-- or unbelief. He knew His Daddy loved Him, and that equipped and empowered Him to live an abundant life. He literally lived in the love of God.

See, the problem with our faith is that it is oftentimes from the outside in. If things are going good, then we believe that God loves us. Or if we are behaving ourselves, we believe that God loves us. But if the opposite appears to be true, then our faith goes out the window. We blame God for everything that goes wrong. We say things like, "God must really hate me because of this, this, and this." We define our God according to our circumstances, rather than defining our circumstances according to the Word of God.

We think "having faith," means believing in something. And in a way it does. As long as what you're believing in is Jesus. But we use it as positive mental assent. We use faith as hope. We hope things will get better and call that faith. Faith is specific though.

Hebrews 11:1, *"Now faith is the substance of things hoped for, the evidence of things not seen."*

First things first... faith is now. Faith is Jesus. Faith isn't in your future, it's in your past. You don't put faith in what you hope WILL happen. You put your faith in what happened on the cross.

Faith is the SUBSTANCE of things hoped for. It is the realization of hope. But let me say it this way: Faith is not what WE hope for. It is what GOD hoped for!

Remember that Jesus is our propitiation, or our atonement? That word also means "wrath appeasement." And that's what Romans 5:9 says, *"More more then, being now justified by his blood, we shall be saved from wrath through him."* But watch this: Wrath is number 3709 in Strong's Greek Concordance and it means, "desire, violent passion." So what if instead of saving us from God's anger... what if Jesus saved us from God's desire?

And God's desire has always been for us to be His people and for Him to be our God. So what if Jesus saved us from God's desire... by fulfilling that desire? What if God's not out to get us, because 2,000 years ago on the cross He got us?

God desired a place to live. He desired a way to get to man. To get INTO man. And Jesus is that Way. Jesus is that Truth. Jesus is that Life. No man comes to the Father except through Jesus, because the Father came to US through Jesus!

Faith is the substance of what was hoped for. It is the fulfillment of God's desire. It is the realization of our EPIC destiny!

Hebrews 11:1, *"Now faith is the substance of things hoped for, the evidence of things not seen."*

Faith is the EVIDENCE of things not seen. And what is not seen... but God? Until He was seen in Jesus. Jesus told Phillip, "If you've seen me you've seen the Father." Colossians 1:15 describes Jesus as *"...the image of the invisible God, the firstborn of every creature."*

See, Jesus doesn't just give us faith... He IS our faith. It's so important what you put your faith in. What you believe in. It is literally the difference between light and darkness, or life and death.

Mark 11:22, *"And Jesus answering saith unto them, Have faith in God."*

In that same way that if it's not love it's not God... if it's not God it's not faith. Jesus was telling us how faith works. We don't have faith in circumstances, or what we see and hear and feel. We have faith in God. 2 Corinthians 5:7 tells us that *"...we walk by faith, not by sight."* This is the response: the walk of faith.

We walk in faith by having faith in God. And watch this: When we have faith in God, then the faith OF God takes over! Our faith hooks us to Jesus, and then HIS faith takes over!

Faith is not a blind leap in the dark. And it is not a blind leap in the light. It's not a blind leap at all. We have faith in God because He proves Himself faithful. We trust in God because He proves Himself trustworthy.

Look at Romans 10:7, *"So then faith cometh by hearing, and hearing by the word of God."*

Our faith, or our belief, comes from God, or from having something to believe in! And this is the all our faith needs to do. It needs to get us to Jesus. Period. In the same way that the Law's true purpose is to get us to realize that we can't do it and we need Jesus... faith's true purpose is to get us to trust in Jesus.

Romans 12:3 says, *"For I say, through the grace given unto me, to every man that is among you, not to think of himself more highly than he ought to think; but to think soberly, according as God hath dealt to every man the measure of faith."*

THE measure of faith. God has given us everything we need. He blessed us with all spiritual blessings. He gave us all things pertaining to life and godliness. He gave us the mind of Christ. He gave us the Holy Spirit. He gave us grace. And He gave us THE measure of faith.

I hear people say, "I need more faith," and I just shake my head. We don't need more faith. We have it all. What we need is to UNDERSTAND our faith. We need to understand what we've been given. We don't need more conforming. We need to understand what we've been conformed into.

Look at what Ephesians 4:13 says, *"Till we all come in the unity of faith, and of the knowledge of the Son of God, unto a perfect man, unto the measure of the stature of the fulness of Christ."*

The unity of faith is the knowledge of the Son of God! Faith IS Jesus!

And this unity of faith, this knowledge of Jesus, transforms us into a perfect man. It fills us up with what we are full of--the stature of the fulness of Christ. It SHOWS us the image that we have been conformed into. And when we SEE it, we will BE it!

Let me give you an example of whose faith it is that is really important. This is the other, "Speaking of Jesus" story I hinted about earlier. It is found in the book of Mark chapter nine.

"And one of the multitude answered and said, Master, I have brought unto thee my son, which hath a dumb spirit; And wheresoever he taketh him, he teareth him: and he foameth, and gnasheth with his

teeth, and pineth away: and I spake to thy disciples that they should cast him out; and they could not. He answereth him, and saith, O faithless generation, how long shall I be with you? how long shall I suffer you? bring him unto me. And they brought him unto him: and when he saw him, straightaway the spirit tare him; and he fell on the ground, and wallowed foaming. And he asked his father, How long is it ago since this came unto him? And he said, Of a child. And ofttimes it hath cast him into the fire, and into the waters, to destroy him: but if thou canst do anything, have compassion on us, and help us. Jesus said unto him, If thou canst believe, all things are possible to him that believeth. And straightway the father of the child cried out, and said with tears, Lord, I believe; help thou mine unbelief. When Jesus saw that the people came running together, he rebuked the foul spirit, saying unto him, Thou dumb and deaf spirit, I charge thee, come out of him, and enter no more into him" (Mark 9:17-25).

Now the first thing we see is that the disciples couldn't help this man. And Jesus called them a faithless generation. He was right there in the midst of them and they didn't get it. They were still trying to DO things, instead of believing in Jesus.

Next we see the father's desperate plea, "...but if thou canst do any thing, have compassion on us." And Jesus' answer, "If thou canst believe, all things are possible to him that believeth." Which we preach as, "If the father had more faith, it could have happened. Or if the disciples had more faith, they could have cast out the spirit." We immediately go to a place of works and labor where the emphasis is on what WE are doing.

But here's the thing to always remember and realize: When Jesus spoke... He was speaking of Himself.

Look at Mark 9:23 in the Amplified Bible, *"And Jesus said, [You say to Me], If You can do anything? [Why,] all things can be (are possible) to him who believes!"* Jesus wasn't saying, "If you can believe then it's possible." Jesus wasn't telling the man what to do. He was offended that the man DIDN'T believe in Him!

162

Jesus said, "What do you mean IF I can do anything? All things are possible to Him who believes!" And Him who believes... is Jesus! All things are possible... to Jesus!

Philippians 4:13 says, *"I can do all things through Christ which strengtheneth me."* I can do all things... THROUGH CHRIST. Because Christ can do all things in and through me! I don't need to do anything, except believe. My response is faith. Period. I step into my EPIC destiny by believing that Jesus brought my EPIC destiny to fulfillment on the cross. I don't conform, I let Jesus show me what I've been conformed into. I don't have faith in anything except Jesus.

And that was the father's response. He said, *"...Lord, I believe; help thou mine unbelief."* He hooked his faith to Jesus. He said, "I believe in you, now you do the rest."

The next verse says, *"When Jesus saw that the people came running together, he rebuked the foul spirit, saying unto him, Thou dumb and deaf spirit, I charge thee, come out of him, and enter no more into him."* As soon as the father hooked his faith to Jesus, Jesus did what the situation called for. The man didn't conqueror the foul spirit. He simply got in the ark. He wasn't a conqueror, he was MORE than a conqueror.

Jesus helped the father's unbelief by giving him something to believe in. He didn't say, "Have more faith." He didn't say, "Do this, this, and this." He said, "All things are possible to Him that believes." He said, "Believe in Me and I've got it covered." This is what verses like 1 Peter 5:7 are talking about (*"Casting all your care upon him; for he careth for you).* They don't mean whine and cry to Jesus, and magnify the problem. They mean TRUST Jesus, because He's got your back.

Jesus not only gives us faith... He IS our faith.

Jesus not only IS the Way, but He KEEPS us on the way. Jude 1:24 describes Jesus in this way, *"Now unto him that is able to keep you from falling, and to present you faultless before the presence of his glory with exceeding joy."* Jesus is able to keep your faith from falling. He is able to keep you on the path. He is the Word that is a light unto our path and a lamp unto our feet.

Jesus is not only the way of grace, but He is the One doing the walk of faith! He's walking in us. Talking in us. Living and loving in us!

Paul said the life I live in the flesh I live by the faith OF the Son of God. It's not even my faith. It's His faith. He gave me THE measure of faith, and that measure is enough to allow me to say, "Lord I believe, help my unbelief." And as soon as I hitch my wagon to Jesus, so to speak, as soon as I get in the Ark (that's already in me) then HIS faith takes over and He lives His life in and through me.

Friends, we were not called to be world changers, or history makers. We were called to be sons. Or, more specifically, we were called to be THE Son. This is our EPIC destiny. This is our Eternal Purpose In Christ. And we live this life by the faith OF the Son of God. We live Jesus' life by letting Jesus live His life in us.

The abundant, everlasting, eternal, Resurrection Life that Jesus came to give us isn't something that we have to do all by ourselves. In fact, it's not something we CAN do all by ourselves. With man it is impossible. Without faith it is impossible to please God. But with God all things are possible.

God conformed us to the image of His Son 2,000 years ago on the cross. But before He did that, he marked us. And I think that's an important topic to look at.

Chapter 17

Marked

I'm pretty sure the first thing we think of, Biblically, when we think of a mark is the mark of the beast. And I'm going to get to that. But before we look at what we have actually been conformed into, and before we look at the mark of the beast, I think we should look at the mark of God.

The mark of God? What in the world is that? Maybe you're more familiar with it being called the mark of Cain.

Genesis 4:15 is the first time the word "mark" is used in the King James Bible. And by the law of first mention, that makes it important. Here's the story: Cain slew his brother Able because he was mad that God rejected his offering and accepted Able's. Cain offered the fruit of the ground. He didn't offer the fruit that God produced--love--but the fruit that he produced--human effort. And God wasn't interested in it.

Able, on the other hand, offered a Lamb. He gave God the only thing God is interested in; Jesus. God is not interested in what we can produce. He's interested in what His Son produced in us. Period.

So Cain, out of jealousy, kills his brother. Let's pick up the story in Genesis chapter 4, verses 9-14. *"And the LORD said unto Cain, Where is Abel thy brother? And he said, I know not: Am I my brother's keeper? And he said, What hast thou done? the voice of thy brother's blood crieth unto me from the ground. And now art thou cursed from the earth, which hath opened her mouth to receive thy brother's blood from thy*

165

hand; When thou tillest the ground, it shall not henceforth yield unto thee her strength; a fugitive and a vagabond shalt thou be in the earth. And Cain said unto the LORD, My punishment is greater than I can bear. Behold, thou hast driven me out this day from the face of the earth; and from thy face shall I be hid; and I shall be a fugitive and a vagabond in the earth; and it shall come to pass, that every one that findeth me shall slay me. And the LORD said unto him, Therefore whosoever slayeth Cain, vengeance shall be taken on him sevenfold. And the LORD set a mark upon Cain, lest any finding him should kill him."

The story of Cain is the story of man. It is the story of trying to please God through our actions, finding that we cannot perform up to the required standard, and turning on the One who could. But it also the story of God. It is a redemption story. The only story ever told: God created man, man messed up and ran from God, and God took care of man regardless.

God said, "If anyone punishes you, vengeance shall be taken on him sevenfold." But we've been punishing and killing each other literally since the day of Cain. We see someone doing something we don't like, and we think we need to be Kingdom cops and set the wrong right.

This was never what God intended though. Our EPIC destiny is NOT to struggle, and fight, and try to conquer evil. Romans 12:21 says, *"Be not overcome of evil, but overcome evil with good."* And this is our mindset: Love the sinner, but hate the sin. Purge the evil. Destroy the darkness. Fight against everything, win the fight, and then rest.

But look at the two verses above Romans 12:21, *"Dearly beloved, avenge not yourselves, but rather give place unto wrath: for it is written, Vengeance is mine; I will repay, saith the Lord. Therefore if thine enemy hunger, feed him; if he thirst, give him drink: for in so doing thou shalt heap coals of fire on his head."*

The coals of fire are embers of the consuming fire that is love. Love is what melts people's hearts. Hate won't change anything or anybody. Jesus didn't fight back when He was accused, or beaten. He laid His life down for His friends. And because He did it a different way--showing us a more excellent way--He purified us with the fire.

Paul said you overcome evil with good. But when he was telling us what that "good" was, he was practically quoting Jesus from Matthew chapter 25. And, as always, Jesus wasn't telling us things to do. He was telling us who He is and what He did. He wasn't telling us to love. He was telling us HOW to love.

Love wins. In fact, love WON 2,000 years ago. History--HIS story--is not about punishment. It is about love. Look what God actually said regarding the mark of Cain, *"And the LORD set a mark upon Cain, lest any finding him should kill him"* (Genesis 4:14). He marked Cain so that everybody else would know that Cain was off limits. He didn't mark Cain so people would know he was bad. He marked Cain so people would know he was... God's.

All throughout the Old Testament the Bible speaks of a remnant of God's people. No matter what happened, no matter if the people of Israel were in bondage, or decimated by their enemies, or what, God always had a witness. He always had a people. He always had a Man.

This is pictured in Noah and his family. It is picked up on in Isaiah 1:9 regarding Abraham's nephew Lot, *"Except the LORD of hosts had left unto us a very small remnant, we should have been as Sodom, and we should have been like unto Gomorrah."*

No matter what, God had a remnant, or a people, or a Man (Jesus), marked out to Himself and for Himself.

Isaiah 11:16 makes this promise, *"And there shall be an highway for the remnant of his people, which shall be left, from Assyria; like as it was to Israel in the day that he came up out of the land of Egypt."* This is the highway of holiness from Isaiah 35:8. This is the Way. This is Jesus.

So when Cain was marked, it wasn't bad. It was good. It was God showing love and grace and mercy. Guys... that's all God can show. Because that's who God is!

So when we think of Cain, what we should think about is God's mark. Not what Cain did, but how God responded to it. Cain said his punishment was too much to bear. And God gave him mercy.

That's the first mark. God's mark. And it trumps the other mark. Where sin abounded, grace much more abounded. God's mark trumps the mark of the beast.

The mark of the beast is used exclusively in the book of Revelation. So let's make this clear before we go any further: Revelation is about the cross. It's not about something that's going to happen. It's about something that happened 2,000 years ago. It's the Revelation of Jesus Christ.

Ok. Revelation 13:11-18, *"And I beheld another beast coming up out of the earth; and he had two horns like a lamb, and he spake as a dragon. And he exerciseth all the power of the first beast before him, and causeth the earth and them which dwell therein to worship the first beast, whose deadly wound was healed. And he doeth great wonders, so that he maketh fire come down from heaven on the earth in the sight of men, And deceiveth them that dwell on the earth by the means of those miracles which he had power to do in the sight of the beast; saying to them that dwell on the earth, that they should make an image to the beast, which had the wound by a sword, and did live. And he had power to give life unto the image of the beast, that the image of the beast should both speak, and cause that as many as would not worship the image of the beast should be killed. And he causeth all, both small and great, rich and poor, free and bond, to receive a mark in their right hand, or in their foreheads: And that no man might buy or sell, save he that had the mark, or the name of the beast, or the number of his name. Here is wisdom. Let him that hath understanding count the number of the beast: for it is the number of a man; and his number is Six hundred threescore and six."*

Let's unravel this. There's a beast, and he has a number. His number is 666 and it's the number of a man. There are only two men that have ever lived: Adam and Jesus. The beast... is Adam. It's the beast nature. The sin nature.

I got this revelation from my pastor so I want to make sure I give him credit for it. Romans is the sixth book in the New Testament. So Romans 6:6 is 666. Romans 6:6 reads, *"Knowing this, that our old man is crucified with him, that the body of sin might be destroyed, that henceforth we should not serve sin."*

The beast... defeated. Our old nature, the sin, or beast nature, destroyed. And look at where it happened. It happened on the cross when Jesus was crucified both for me and as me. It happened when I was crucified. It happened in water baptism.

And look at John 6:66, another 666, *"From that time many of his disciples went back, and walked no more with him."*

The beast... is Adam. It is the unregenerated mind. The carnal mind. And the mark of the beast is in the forehead and the hand. It is in our thoughts and our actions!

Revelation 13:11 says that the beast comes up out of the earth. Adam was made of the dust of the earth. And anything coming up-- anything trying to ascend--is doomed to fail. This is what happened with Adam, and with Cain, and with the tower of Babel... man tried to get to God. It never works.

Man can't get to God. Even obeying the Law doesn't get us there. Trying to obey the Law only reveals that "one thing you lack." And the one thing we lack--in that economy, before the cross--is the Holy Spirit. We're marked in the forehead and the hand by the mark of the beast.

The cross, and the Passover Lamb that pointed to the cross, marked us in another way. *"For the LORD will pass through to smite the Egyptians; and when he seeth the blood upon the lintel, and on the two side posts, the LORD will pass over the door, and will not suffer the destroyer to come in unto your houses to smite you"* (Exodus 12:23).

The blood of the Lamb was applied to the top of the door (the lintel) and the two side posts. It was applied to your mind and your actions. It was applied to the forehead and the hand!

And it marked you in exactly the same way as the mark of Cain! The mark of Cain told people they were not allowed to smite Cain. The blood of the Lamb told the destroyer not to smite you! It's the same mark and the same story.

But it didn't spare you from death. The firstborn HAD to die. Adam, the old man, had to go. That's the part where we understand that we were crucified with Christ. The blood didn't tell the destroyer to skip your house because a death wasn't necessary. The blood told the destroyer to skip your house because the death had already taken place! Jesus' death was our death! The old man died on the cross!

The problem that we find so often is that we're dragging around a corpse. We think we bear the mark of the beast, and that's how we act. We don't believe there is no spot in us, we don't believe that the work is finished. And that sin (or unbelief) causes us to act like we've got spots. It causes us to act like sinners.

We think we bear the mark of the beast, and we think we are the image of the beast. Revelation 13:15, *"And he had the power to give life unto the image of the beast, that the image of the beast should both speak, and cause that as many as would not worship the image of the beast should be killed."*

The wrong image speaks to us. It whispers in our ear and it uses the Law to back up what it's saying. It says, "How can you say you're a Christian when you just did this, this, and this? Only a sinner would do this, this, and this."

And guess who gives it that power? WE DO! What we behold is what we become. What we magnify is what manifests. What we believe is what is real to us.

The beast tells you that you are what you do. The voice of Truth tells you that you are who Jesus is. And whichever one you believe, that's which one is real in your life.

So what do we do? There are two marks in play, the mark of God and the mark of the beast. Well, we've seen that the beast was put to death on the cross. We've seen that the blood of the Lamb and the Word of our testimony (which is Jesus) has caused us to overcome. We've seen that Jesus did it all so we could get it all.

So what do we do? Romans 6:11, *"Likewise reckon ye also yourselves to be dead indeed unto sin, but alive unto God through Jesus Christ our Lord."* We RECKON ourselves. "Reckon" is G3049 in Strong's Concordance. It means, "to take an inventory." It means, to take your temperature. To see what's what.

And Revelation 11:1-2 gives us the vital key. *"And there was given me a reed like unto a rod: and the angel stood, saying, Rise, and measure the temple of God, and the altar, and them that worship therein. But the court which is without the temple leave out, and measure it not; for it is given unto the Gentiles: and the holy city shall they tread under foot forty and two months."*

We measure the temple with the reed that's like unto a rod. We are the temple. We measure ourselves with the reed that is like unto a rod. Matthew chapter 12 speaks of a prophecy that was spoken by Isaiah. A prophecy being fulfilled in Jesus. And it describes Jesus as a bruised reed. Jeremiah 10:16 says it like this, *"The portion of Jacob is not like them: for he is the former of all things; and Israel is the rod of his inheritance: The LORD of hosts is his name."*

Jesus is the rod that is like unto a reed! We measure ourselves by Jesus!

The angel told John NOT to measure the outer court. NOT to measure the outer man. To know no man (including ourselves) after the flesh. It's not what you do that defines you. It's who you ARE that defines you. It's who lives in you that defines you.

We don't have to die to sin. We already did that when Jesus did it for us and as us. We don't need to get rid of our spots, or our wrinkles. Jesus already did that and presented us to Himself as His bride. We don't need to get rid of the mark of the beast, because Jesus did that when He gave us HIS mark.

See... we were created in the image of God, but we thought we had the mark and the image of the beast. That was never our destiny though. Our EPIC Destiny was to be conformed into the image of Jesus. And that's what happened on the cross.

So just what exactly IS the image that we were conformed into?

Chapter 18

The Image

Romans 8:29, *"For whom he did foreknow, he also did predestinate to be conformed to the image of his Son, that he might be the firstborn among many brethren."* This, in a nutshell, is our EPIC destiny. It is our Eternal Purpose In Christ. It is why we are here. But what, exactly, IS the image of God's Son? What, exactly, HAVE we been conformed into?

I can sum it up in one verse: *"And the Holy Ghost descended in a bodily shape like a dove upon him, and a voice came from heaven, which said, Thou art my beloved Son; in thee am I well pleased"* (Luke 3:22). This says it. The image that we have been conformed into... is beloved. And the Holy Spirit--our love receptor--is what shows us what the image is. The Holy Spirit is what allows us to see ourselves as Jesus. It is what allows us to "be loved."

The difference, at its most basic level, between Adam and Jesus is that Adam didn't know God loved him. Adam was the son of God, but he wasn't the Beloved Son of God. Not because God didn't love him, but because he couldn't receive it.

Jesus is God in the flesh. He is literally love in a body. He received God's love and released God's love like nobody else ever had, because Jesus was filled with the Holy Spirit. He had a love receptor that nobody else ever had. Everybody before the cross was in a cursed dimension of working hard and earning everything by the sweat of their brow.

Jesus reversed the curse by sweating great drops of blood. His blood redeemed us. And by completely identifying with us, by becoming sin, He allowed us to completely identify with Him! He made us the righteousness of God. He conformed us into His image. He gave us His Spirit. The Spirit of Truth. Our love receptor. He filled that God-shaped hole inside of us, by filling us with Himself!

God is love, but see, that doesn't mean anything if you don't see Him that way. Look at this story in Matthew chapter 16 verses 13-18, *"When Jesus came into the coasts of Caesarea Philippi, he asked his disciples, saying, Whom do men say that I the Son of man am? And they said, Some say that thou art John the Baptist: some, Elias; and others, Jeremias, or one of the prophets. He saith unto them, But whom say ye that I am? And Simon Peter answered and said, Thou art the Christ, the Son of the living God. And Jesus answered and said unto him, Blessed art thou, Simon Barjona: for flesh and blood hath not revealed it unto thee, but my Father which is in heaven. And I say also unto thee, That thou art Peter, and upon this rock I will build my church; and the gates of hell shall not prevail against it."*

Who do you say that Jesus is? That's really the most important question you'll ever have to answer. Because how you see God is how you relate to God. If you see Him as an angry taskmaster who is out to get you every time you mess up and break that Law... you'll run away from Him. But if you see Him as a loving heavenly Father... you'll run to Him.

John 3:35 defines our relationship with God. *"The Father loveth the Son, and hath given all things into his hand."*

This is why we are here. We are here so that God could love us. That is our EPIC destiny. We're not here to DO. We're here to BE. And more accurately... we're here to be loved.

Jesus is God's beloved Son. That is the image that we were conformed into. That means WE are God's beloved Son. We are Jesus, because Jesus drew us all into Himself, and transformed us all into Himself.

This is so important because if you believe that the Father loveth the Son... and you believe that you ARE the Son... then you can believe that the Father has given all things into your hand.

It's easy to believe that the Father loves Jesus. And it's easy to believe that the Father gave all things into His hand. But all of THAT believing doesn't do anything for US.

It's easy to believe that there's no separation between the Father and the Son. Jesus said, *"I and my Father are one"* (John 10:30). And Jesus told Phillip, "If you've seen me, you've seen the Father."

The hard part seems to be seeing that WE and JESUS are one. Seeing that there is no separation between Father and Son... and we are the Son!

Jesus said it like this, *"At that day ye shall know that I am in my Father, and ye in me, and I in you"* (John 14:20).

I know it's hard though. It's a mystery. In fact, that's exactly what Colossians 1:27 said it was, *"To whom God would make known what is the riches of the glory of this mystery among the Gentiles; which is Christ in you, the hope of glory."* The mystery is Christ in us. The image is Christ in us. It's all about us understanding that we are in Him--we ARE Him--because He is in us!

And Colossians speaks of the riches of the glory. These are the "all things" that the Father gave into the Son's hand. Blessed with all spiritual blessings. Given all things that pertain to life and godliness. All things. All truth.

Love.

God gave us everything when He gave us Himself. He gave us His love, and His Spirit allows us to receive what we've been given. It allows us to let this mind of Christ that's in us BE in us. It's allows us to let God love us. It empowers us to BE beloved! To be who we really are. It shows us the image that we have been conformed into, by showing us the true image of God!

After Peter correctly identified Jesus, Jesus told Him, "That revelation came straight from Daddy." And then He said He was going to build His church on that rock. Not on Peter's faith, but on the revelation of who He is! The revelation of who He is... in us! The revelation of who we are!

There's nothing in this life more important than knowing that God loves you. Knowing that He is YOUR Father, and YOU are His beloved Son. Knowing that God is well pleased with you, and that it has nothing to do with your actions.

Your actions aren't the issue. Sin isn't the issue. (But that's another book altogether.) The issue is knowing who you are, where you are, and why you're here. And you are here to be loved. Period.

Knowing that you are loved doesn't change your appetite, but it allows your appetite to be satisfied. It allows you to receive love from the Father and stop looking for it in all the wrong places. It allows you to stop being who you think God wants you to be, and simply be who you truly are.

I preach this a lot, but shining the light doesn't change anything. If you're in a dark and messy room, and you turn the light on, you're still in a messy room. All the light does is reveal things as they truly are.

The light of Jesus that shines in our hearts reveals that God's heart beats in our chest! And God's heart beats with love. We are the beloved Son because the Holy Spirit--the Truth of the matter--allows us to be loved. The light allows us to see God as He truly is, and in that mirror we see ourselves as we truly are!

Before there was anything there was God the Father and Jesus the Son. And the Father loved the Son. But love is too big to contain. One

Son wasn't enough to hold all that love. It filled Jesus up and came exploding out of Him. The River was too big to be bottled up.

And that's where the "firstborn among many brethren" part of Romans 8:29 comes in. Jesus came in the flesh and dwelt among us. God's love lived in a man. In a body. But it was too big. So Jesus drew us into Himself and made us a part of that New Man. He made us members of the Body of Christ. He took who He is and filled us up with it. He transformed us into who is. He conformed us into His image.

Now we can rest, because the work is finished. We don't have to earn anything from God. Everything God has and everything God is was freely given when Jesus offered Himself on the cross. And everything that God has and everything that God is... is love.

God always loved us, but He needed a way to GET that love to us. He needed to plant something inside of us. A clean heart and an upright spirit. His heart, and His Holy Spirit.

Jesus died so we could die. So that mark of the beast, and all of the sin and death that we were in bondage to, could be washed away. And then Jesus rose again so we could live. But the only way that works is with Him living in and through us.

Before the cross is was all about religion. Because that's all we could understand. We thought we could earn love though our behavior. We thought if we tried hard enough, if we got enough knowledge of good and evil, we could stop doing evil and start doing good. And we thought if we did good we would be accepted.

After the cross--where we are now--it's not about religion at all. It's about relationship. It's not about laws you keep, it's about a life that keeps you. And relationships are all about connection. They are all about intimacy, and trust. Relationships... are all about love.

Hebrews 13:1 in the Message Bible says, *"Stay on good terms with each other, held together by love."*

It's so simple, but so powerful. We are held together by love. Everything is held together by love. We thought God was mad at us, that He didn't love us, and everything fell apart. We couldn't believe right, so we couldn't behave right. We ran from God, and hid from His presence. We couldn't come to God, and we really didn't want to.

So God came to us.

God BECAME us.

And then, through the cross, we became Him.

God planted Himself in corruption so that He could raise us in incorruption. He fought the fight because we couldn't win it. He did the work because we couldn't do it. He made a New Covenant with Himself, and included us in it by our faith.

He circumcised us, and anointed us. He washed us clean with His blood. He transformed us. But He didn't transform us into something He could love. He always loved us. He transformed us into something that could RECEIVE His love.

Jesus received God's love. Jesus is the Father's beloved Son. Jesus knew who He was, and where He was, and why He was there.

And He conformed us into that same image. He made us His brethren, the members or parts of His body. He made us... Him.

Jesus was God in the flesh. He was a man with the Holy Spirit. That's who He was. And that's who we are. (See Identity Crisis)

Jesus is heaven on earth. He's in the Throne because He is the Throne. He is the Promised Land called rest. And that's where we are. (See Six Steps to the Throne)

Jesus was loved by the Father. Everything He said, and everything He did, and everything He was, came from that love. That's why we're here. That's our EPIC destiny.

To be loved by God. That's it. There's nothing greater than that. That's our Eternal Purpose In Christ. This whole Christian journey, this Resurrection Life, is all about getting to the heart of the matter. And the heart of the matter is God's heart. The heart of the matter is God's love beating in our chests.

We do what we do because of who we are. I'm a writer, that's why I write. I'm God's love, that's why I love.

Jesus did what He did because He was moved with compassion and motivated by love. He knew that love holds everything together. So when He saw something that looked like it was broken, He bound it up with love. When He saw sickness... love healed it. When He saw bondage... love freed it.

Everywhere He went, Jesus made things on earth how they are in heaven. He literally brought heaven to earth, by bringing God's love to earth. And in the same way, that's what we do. That's why we're here.

God's love fills us up. We receive it and release it. And watch this: The scientific definition of, "full" is, "overflowing." If we're full of God's love--and because we've been conformed into the image of His Son we ARE full of His love--that means it's overflowing. That means it's coming out of us all on its own.

We don't produce the fruit. We simply bear it. We simply feast on it and dwell in it. We simply believe that it's true.

The way of grace made it all possible. The walk of faith takes God at His Word and believes that it's true.

I want to close this book by simply saying that our EPIC destiny is not to DO anything... except be who we are. Not to DO anything... except let God love us. Because when we do that, everything else flows naturally.

You don't have to try to be somebody you're not. In fact, that's what Paul warned against when he wrote, *"And be not conformed to this world: but be ye transformed by the renewing of your mind, that ye may prove what is that good, and acceptable, and perfect, will of God"* (Romans 12:2).

You HAVE been conformed into the image of Jesus. You CAN see yourself as the beloved Son of God. The key is renewing your mind. The key is not conforming back to the world. Don't go back. Don't believe the lie.

The truth has set you free and made you free.

Free to run, and free to dance...

Free to be loved, and free to love.

Amen.

About the Author

Pastor Tom Carter is the founder of Word Without Walls Ministry. He lives in Waterford MI, with his son, Logan. He is the author of two other Jesus books, *Identity Crisis,* and *Six Steps to the Throne,* and the fictional super hero Capa City Novels, *Crystal Star,* and *Hazard.* He has a Bachelor's Degree in Theology from Destiny Christian University. He blogs (or Rants) daily on his website: www.jesusrant.com The first year of Jesus Rants are collected in a year-long daily devotional, *Jesus Rant Vol. 1.*

The Jesus Rant

The Jesus Rant is just that: a daily blog (or Rant) about Jesus. Pastor Tom reflects on events in his life and reveals fresh revelations from the Lord. The entire Bible speaks of Jesus, every book and every chapter. It's all about Jesus. If you don't see Jesus, you're looking at it wrong. It is Pastor Tom's calling to shine the light of Jesus into a dark world, to be a lighthouse, and shine forth a Revolution of Revelation. Follow Pastor Tom on www.jesusrant.com